FOOTPRINTS
IN THE SOIL

FOOTPRINTS IN THE SOIL

A Portuguese-Californian Remembers

ROSE PETERS EMERY

may 4, 2003

For Gary,

with warm regards and
my very best wishes.
Rose Peters Emery

PORTUGUESE HERITAGE PUBLICATIONS

SAN JOSE, CALIFORNIA

for Helen

Portuguese Heritage Publications of California
P.O. Box 32517
San Jose, CA 95152

Book and cover design: Lisa Schulz/Elysium, San Francisco
Cover photo: Dianne Hagaman

First Edition.
Printed in the USA.

07 06 05 04 03   5 4 3 2 1

ISBN: 0-9728576-0-5
Library of Congress Cataloging-in-Publication Data
available from the publisher.
Library of Congress Control Number: 2003102002
For additional books please contact:
Craftsman Distributors
1173 Singletary Avenue
San Jose, CA 95126

Contents

Acknowledgements

This memoir began as pages filled with miscellaneous notes and short sketches, jotted down as I remembered them. Several years of expanding, rewriting, and reshaping finally resulted in a book, but not without help and encouragement from others all along the way. I would like to thank: the members of the writing class at the San Francisco Senior Center and especially our teacher, Toni Mester, for consistent encouragement and perceptive criticism; Dianne Hagaman for her cover photograph; Ralph Cozine for sharing his knowledge of San Ramon Valley history and for generous and invaluable aid with photographs; Arlene Kaplan Daniels for her advocacy on my behalf; Tony Goulart for his advice on publishing; Marillyn Cozine for eagle-eyed proofreading; Art Carroll for immigration research; Joyce Nicholas and Molly Threipland for thoughtful comments; and Gilda Bettencourt, Joanne Vâs Camara, Deolinda Avila, and Ron Duarte for helpful kindness.

My family has been my inspiration and mainstay. My niece, Sylvia Carroll, helped in countless ways and her enthusiasm for my project has been unflagging. It was Sylvia who convinced me to take a first trip to the Azores at the age of 86. My grandchildren Mark Giambruni and Kim Giambruni Kenin, my great-grandson Joshua Murray, and my niece Gertrude Peters Rodriguez provided loving encouragement. My son-in-law, Eliot Freidson, answered many questions about computers. But my biggest debt is to my daughter, Helen Giambruni, for her invaluable help in coordinating, word processing and editing this book. Without her I would not have completed it.

Preface

THIS IS THE STORY of my Portuguese-American family—
my immigrant father, my American-born mother and my
eleven brothers and sisters—and of the grain and cattle ranch
in the San Ramon Valley of California that was the center of all
our lives.

I am a very old woman but luckily my memory is as good
as ever. My years on the ranch are still vivid in my mind. About
six years ago I decided to write a history of those years so our
family stories would not disappear with me and so my great-
grandson and his wife could pass them on to their children. In
this book I have tried to set down all that I was told of my parents' early lives and what I remember from those years before
1923 when I was still at home.

We were luckier than many other immigrant families
because my father came to this country at a time when he
could homestead good farmland, and both my parents had
farming skills. They also had some old-fashioned virtues that
are now often devalued: hard work, diligence, thrift, honesty.
My family happens to be of Portuguese descent but many
other immigrant groups have come to the United States hoping for a better life for their families and willing to work and
sacrifice to achieve it. More are still coming. Like the
Portuguese, these others have sometimes met with prejudice
and misunderstanding. I honor them, too, in writing this story
of my parents and their achievements.

FOOTPRINTS IN THE SOIL

The Home Ranch

OTHER PEOPLE REFERRED to our family's 256-acre ranch in the San Ramon Valley of California as the Peters Ranch. We always called it "the Home Ranch" to distinguish it from the Butcher and Palmer ranches that my parents also owned. Certainly to the family it seemed an ideal home. From the large flat and the gently rounded areas that bordered the roadway, the land gradually sloped upward by means of rolling hills toward the wooded Las Trampas Range that bordered its west side and provided firewood for our stove and heater. A fence not far from the edge of the woods separated the steep, untillable area from the rest of the land. In alternate years, the tillable land was planted to grain (wheat, mostly, with some oats and barley), then used as pasturage for cattle so as not to wear out the soil. Two widely separated deep gullies started some 300 feet below the fence and stretched downward toward the road, effectively dividing the land into three workable strips. The small creeks in the gullies carried off a lot of water in the rainy season but dried up in summer.

The existing ranch house was a fairly large, one-story white clapboard building, sound but plain, having no particular style. Together with the "bunkhouse" in the back yard (so

Calf roundup, the Peters Home Ranch, San Ramon, California, about 1920. One of two gullies in background.

called because it was originally built for hired hands), the house was big enough for the nine to eleven of us who lived there between 1905 and 1923, the years I was growing up. Besides Mama and Papa there were five of us children from Papa's second family (his first wife had died years before,

The Peters farmhouse, about 1930.

leaving him with seven children). The eldest of us, born in 1898, was Arthur, who was called "Tiny" all his life by everyone except his teachers. I never heard who gave him that nickname or why—perhaps he was especially small as a baby. When grown, he was short, about 5' 5", but that was the usual height for men in our family. In any case, he never gave any sign that he was troubled in the slightest by the nickname, and the rest of us never thought about it; it was just his name, no different from "Henry" or "John." Albert (Bert) was born in 1900, followed by Edward (Ed) in 1903, by me in 1905 and, finally, by Evelyn in 1907. Another child, little Louie, died of diarrhea in infancy, leaving five of us in all. As the official nickname-inventer of our family, Tiny later named me "Sid," derived from

Evelyn's inability to pronounce "sister" as a toddler, and Evelyn "Nip" from a certain nippiness in her personality. Evelyn's daughter, Sylvia, and her daughter, Juliette, still call me "Aunt Sid." No one else is left who uses that name.

By the time I was a small child, only Frances, the youngest of my older half-brothers and sisters, was still at home. The others had left the farm, all of them except the youngest, Manuel, having married. Somewhat later, after an accident, Manuel returned to live at home. Then there was our cousin, John Soares, the adult son of one of Papa's sisters, who lived with us for a few years when he first came to this country from the Azores. He worked on the ranch until he learned enough English to go off on his own.

A wide, L-shaped veranda served as entrance porch to the ranch house and wrapped around the right corner of the house for about fifteen feet. Nobody in our hardworking family ever thought of taking time out to sit there on the veranda but it made a good place for my sister Evelyn and me to play. There were six main rooms. Between the front and back doors ran the parlor, dining-room and kitchen and along to their left a row of three bedrooms. All the rooms except the parlor and the back bedroom were spacious. Our parlor contained a set of late-Victorian furniture with stiff, tufted, brocade backs and seats and a good deal of fancy carving on the glossy wooden frames. I thought they were beautiful and was unhappy when Mama modernized by ordering from Sears and Roebuck a set of equally stiff Mission-style furniture in brown oak. The room was small, appropriately so, for we certainly didn't use it much. I can only remember anyone in there on those rare occasions when a neighbor or my godmother came to visit.

We always seemed to congregate in the kitchen—not only those of us who lived at home but also any visiting brothers and sisters and extended family. Mama would knead bread, or chop up meat, potatoes and onions in a wooden bowl for hash. We girls would set the table or busy ourselves with stringing beans or peeling potatoes. The smell of roasting beef from the big black wood stove or apple pie fresh from the oven and cooling on the long wooden table would whet our appetites. Some would sit on the bench under the window and one or two of us kids would perch on the covered wood box to the left of the stove, jumping up when Mama needed firewood. The kitchen was always the warmest place in the house, socially and otherwise.

To the right of the stove was the doorway to the dining-room, the biggest room in the house. It was about 12 x 18 feet, long enough to hold not only an extendable eight-foot dining table and chairs and a sewing machine placed under the window for the light but a velour-covered couch where Papa could take his short naps after lunch—with enough room left over to set up a quilting frame when needed. On a plate board above the wainscotting was a mantel clock that Papa wound up every night. This room held the only wall decoration in the house, a big map of California that he had bought from a traveling salesman. A small desk that Bert had made in grammar school woodworking class and a wall telephone completed the room's furnishings. The telephone was an oak box with a bell-shaped mouthpiece, an earphone hung up on a metal holder on the side of the box, and below it a crank that you turned to signal the operator. One long ring and three shorts was our number. Not many people had a telephone in those days but Mama had

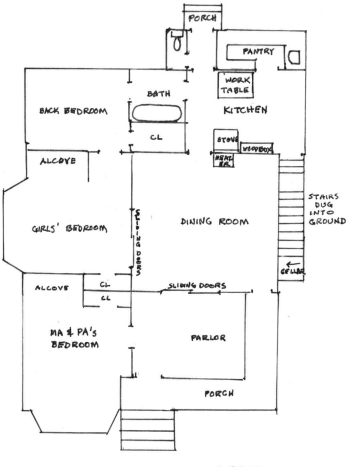

PORCH

PANTRY

BACK BEDROOM

BATH

WORK TABLE

KITCHEN

CL

STOVE

WOODBOX

HEATER

ALCOVE

STAIRS DUG INTO GROUND

GIRLS' BEDROOM

SLIDING DOORS

DINING ROOM

CELLAR

ALCOVE

CL

CL

SLIDING DOORS

MA & PA's BEDROOM

PARLOR

PORCH

THE PETERS FARMHOUSE
c. 1920
SAN RAMON, CA

managed to get her way in this, as she often did on things that really mattered to her. The telephone was a lifeline for an isolated farm. Before its advent, when one of the children was sick and needed medicine she had to have someone stand out in the road and flag down Mrs. Swartz, who lived in San Ramon and drove by in her buggy in the mornings.

Bedrooms were minimally furnished with beds and a bureau for clothes. Closets, one for each bedroom, were small, and clothes hung on hooks rather than on hangers. The front bedroom off the parlor, where Mama and Papa slept, and also the middle bedroom off the dining-room where Frances, Evelyn and I slept, had bay windows and alcoves which added to their floor space. Frances slept on a single bed in the alcove in our bedroom, curtained off for privacy, until she left home sometime in her twenties. Ed slept in the small back room, while our older brothers and Cousin John, or a hired man, slept out back in the bunkhouse.

One of my earliest remembrances is of the coal oil (kerosene) lamps we used for lighting. The coal oil was poured into the base of the lamp, a glass container shaped like a small, round loaf of bread on which the glass globe rested. The opening on top was fitted with a metal gadget into which the flat cotton wick was fed so that it reached down into the kerosene and could be raised or lowered by turning a tiny wheel.

By about 1916, however, we had acetylene gas piped into the house for gas lights. A gas pipe extended down about four feet from the ceiling, at which point it branched out into two arms, whose tapering ends jutted upward to form the jets. When a petcock below the jets was turned on we could get light merely by touching a match to them. No filling, no cleaning of equipment! However, the gas itself wasn't so simple. It was home-produced in a tank-like contraption set up in a corner of the wash house. Carbide, which when mixed with water produced the gas, came in metal drums about four feet high. After the chemical had done its gas-producing work, a lot of thick, white, chalky residue had to be removed from the tank part of the machine and dumped in a part of the orchard which was not in use. Although gas lights were far superior to kerosene lamps, we were even happier when completely work-free, efficient electric lights became available. The good light made sewing and doing our homework a great deal easier. I believe this happened while I was still in grammar school, so it would have been before 1919.

As for heat, a wood-burning heater in the dining-room occupied the wall directly behind the kitchen wood stove, and they shared the same chimney. Together they provided all the warmth in the house. In winter, the bedrooms and bathroom were so cold that Ev and I often went to stand in front of the heater in the dining room while we dressed.

The bathroom, which was located between the kitchen and the back bedroom, contained a long zinc tub in a wooden frame, a washbasin, a small mirror and a roller towel. If you wanted to use it, you pulled it around until you found a dry spot. Fastened to a door casing was the black leather strop that Papa used to sharpen his straight razor. There was no medicine cabinet; Mama kept medicines and laxatives on a shelf in the kitchen. Nor was there any toilet, for Papa was convinced that it would be unsanitary to have one inside the house. The privy was out in the back yard and because no one wanted to go out there in the cold at night, we had chamber pots under all the beds. Once, however, when Pa was away for a few days because he had to testify at a trial, Mama had a plumber put in a flush toilet on the back porch. The story was that Papa refused to use it for some time but one winter night decided to try it, and thereafter continued. Nobody said anything about it to him.

Both the dining-room and kitchen originally had softwood floors that had to be scrubbed with a strong solution of something like Sal Soda to clean and whiten them, but Mama later covered them with inlaid linoleum for easy cleaning. There was an old rug in the parlor, and the master bedroom was always carpeted, but for a long time the other bedroom floors were covered only by thin straw matting. Later Mama ordered three rugs from Sears and Roebuck—a "velvet" one for the parlor and two Axminster types to replace the straw matting in the bedrooms. When these arrived at the San Ramon train depot, Papa picked them up in the spring wagon, so called because the seat rested on springs to make for more comfortable riding.

Our front garden was one of the old-fashioned kind that was typical of the times. There was no lawn, no plan, just a miscellaneous assortment of plants stuck in here and there wherever they happened to fit. Probably most of them had been put in before we bought the property. Leading up from the road, a pathway to the house divided the fenced garden into two unequal parts. A gate in the right fence led to the family orchard, while on the left side a gate opened on to what we called the Big Yard. Hitching posts stood next to both gates. The focal point of the garden, at least until it stopped working and was removed, was a fountain that the previous owners, the Wood family, had constructed. A pipe jutted out of the earth with a sprinkler on top and someone had heaped rocks around it to form a cone six feet in diameter, then covered it all with a layer of dirt. Many small, attractive plants were kept alive by the water.

Roses, our favorite flower, were the most numerous plant. We had large, pink cabbage roses but I loved best the tiny, pink, sweet-smelling baby roses that grew near an oleander. On a trellis that divided the front garden from the back yard and all along the fence that bordered the Big Yard we planted dark red, open-faced climbers. Virginia creeper and fragrant honeysuckle trailed over the wire fence on the orchard side, and white roses grew over the fence in front. In the garden there were lilacs, a mock orange with its sweet-smelling cream flowers and three small fruit trees that Papa must have planted —an orange whose fruit always got frozen, a loquat and a fig. For color there was the red of geraniums, the yellow of daffodils, the purple of violets, the blue of myrtle and the pink of amaryllis.

The back yard was for work and was no-nonsense, hard-packed bare dirt. Across the yard, about twenty feet from the back steps, was the bunkhouse. To the left of it was the wood-shed, and behind it were the smokehouse, the main chicken coop and the privy. The bunkhouse itself was actually a multi-purpose structure. In the far corner was the "meat room," a small room with a bench where Papa would cut up sides of pork. Next to the meat room, in the rear of the building, were the two bedrooms. Across the front of the bunkhouse was an open porch and a large "washroom" or laundry room. The washing was done the old way—scrubbed on a board by hand. However, the presence of piped hot and cold water in the wash house, as well as in the kitchen and bathroom in the main

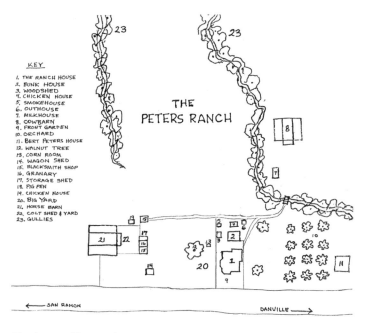

Plan drawing of Peters ranch.

house, was rather luxurious for the time.

All our water came from our own property. Centrally located just below the Las Trampas range was a sulfur spring from which bubbles would continually rise to the surface, releasing a rotten-egg odor. Water from the spring was piped into a trough in the cattle pasture. It was unpleasant to drink but the cattle didn't seem to mind at all.

About 200 yards north of the sulfur spring was a second spring from which we took our own drinking water. This was wholesome but very hard, so that it tasted of minerals and left a thick scum in the dishpan when we washed the dishes. A pipe led down from the spring to a storage reservoir on a slope about halfway to the ranch house. Water for the house was piped from there. Our reservoir was like a small room, walled in with planks. It had a wooden cover and a fence around it to keep the cattle away. That spring was really a fine one for it once provided water for the entire town of Danville, then, of course, very small.

Behind the cow barn was a large vegetable garden. Later, when walnuts became a popular and lucrative crop, this area was a walnut orchard. Papa always planted corn, potatoes and a few peas and string beans, the vegetables he was used to eating. I used to watch him cut up potatoes for planting, with an eye or two on each piece because that's where the sprout would emerge. Once he tried growing the old-country favorites kale and fava beans but none of the rest of us liked them so he gave them up. Only years later did he plant big, juicy beefsteak tomatoes, which grew wonderfully flavorful in our hot, dry summers.

Every year Pa planted cantaloupes and watermelons, which were a treat in those summers. He would wrap some watermelon seeds in a thick, damp cloth and place them on top of the warming oven to sprout, thus getting a head start on the growing season. I remember how all five of us kids— Bert, Tiny, Ed, Ev and I—used to sit in a row on the bunkhouse porch, boys in the bib overalls they always wore, we girls in our gingham dresses, devouring thick slices of watermelon. We would spit out the seeds onto the packed earth of the yard and wait for our red-crested white leghorn chickens to come running and peck them up. These chickens were truly free-range, for they were never cooped up and had the run of the place. (Luckily we almost never went barefoot.) At night, though, they went of their own accord to roost in the hen-house.

Our turkeys never seemed to take to domestication as our chickens did. Perhaps they hadn't yet been bred for it. After all, it hadn't been very long since they were wild birds shot for food by the early settlers moving west. Unlike the chickens, they never roosted indoors, preferring the relative isolation and security of the upper branches of the locust trees that lined the chicken yard fence. They also liked to build nests in secluded places, for example, under the Japanese willow that used to grow in the creek that ran in front of the Big Yard. Harry Hurst once telephoned to report that all of our turkeys were roosting on a fence outside his store, almost a mile away in San Ramon. My brothers must have had a time bringing them home.

Although I only remember our keeping 3 or 4 hogs at a time, tax records show that in 1904 Papa was raising 25. It must have been about then that he grew so much corn for feed that he had to build a special shed, the "corn room," in one corner of the Big Yard to store it in. In later years I remember seeing him take a dry corn cob and rub it against a shucked ear to remove the kernels so they could be used for seed.

What we always called the "Big Yard" was really a huge corral situated between the farmhouse and the horse barn. As the dirt was pounded hard and the grass kept very short by many hoof beats, it served as a large courtyard when free of animals and a baseball field for us kids whenever we wanted to play. Around the yard were located various small farm buildings—the blacksmith and tool shop, the granary, three wagon and farm equipment sheds, the hog pen and the smaller of the two chicken houses. The latter was at some distance from the house, down near the horse barn. One night some thief raided it and made off with every last chicken. Nobody in the house heard a sound and at the time we had no dog to warn us. That theft was the only crime we were ever the victims of, though we never locked a door.

The horse barn was downhill from the house on the San Ramon side of the property. Its front doors were huge, wide and tall enough for a wagon load of hay to be driven through the central passageway. The floor was packed earth. Six or eight heavy draft horses were housed in a row of stalls across the front of the barn on either side of the passage. I still remember their names—Fanny, Wiedie (who was bought from the Wiedemann family), Molly, Sally, Kate, May, Lena and Pete. Lily, the buggy horse, was berthed in a stall at one end and Nelly (later replaced by Captain), the riding horse, at the other end. From a narrow aisle along the front of the stalls, pitchfork loads of hay were thrust into the wooden mangers at the head of each stall. Attached to one end of each manger was a small feed box into which Papa would empty a measured amount of rolled barley. Farther back in the barn, behind both rows of stalls, were ample storage areas that held loose hay for the horses and a big wooden box for the barley.

Sets of harness hung on pegs on the barn wall behind the horses where they were handy to use—hames, tugs, cruppers and the heavy, contoured, pear-shaped horse collars, well padded and lined with soft, smooth leather to keep tender shoulders from chafing. Since a horse with galled shoulders couldn't be worked, great care was taken to avoid the problem. The horses were groomed regularly with currycomb and

Horse barn with cattle round-up in Big Yard, about 1922.

brush and they seemed to greatly enjoy it. On days when they were not working they were turned out into the Big Yard for exercise. How they kicked and cavorted, punctuating their joy with scatterings of manure and rolling over and over to scratch their backs in the hard-to-get-at places!

The cow barn was quite a distance from the house, up behind the bunkhouse. It was a large, square wooden structure, weathered to dark gray. An attached calf shed extended part way across the front and to the left of that was a generous sized barn door. As you entered you found yourself in a wide corridor that extended the length of the barn. There was a floor of wooden planks. Along the right was a row of stanchions, trap-like contraptions through which the cows would thrust their heads to get at the hay-filled mangers in front of them, only to find themselves locked in place so they could be milked. Hay was forked into the mangers from the huge

The cow barn, with milk house at left.

reserve supply which was stored in the rest of the barn. A milk house that held the cream separator was located just outside the fence of the cow corral, near the gate.

Milking machines had not yet come into use so milking was still done by hand. I liked to see to see the row of a dozen or so cows locked in their stanchions, and to watch the milkers at work. When I was very young, about five or six, I would take a cup and walk up to the cow barn to get a cup of milk that was fresh and warm from the cow and so foamy from being squirted into the bucket that it left a foam mustache on my upper lip. Although our cats were never tame, at that time we had one who sometimes dared to come into the barn so that one of the milkers would squirt a stream of milk into its mouth. I remember that the milker, probably Cousin John Soares, sat on a one-legged stool (a *banca,* Papa called it), which had a nail point projecting from the bottom of its leg to prevent his slipping.

Evelyn and I sometimes climbed up to the sulfur spring but we loved even more to walk the nearest gully, the one that ran down behind the cow barn. In winter a small creek ran along its bottom. Its sloping banks were covered with trees. There was the live oak with its prickly dark green leaves and the laurel or California bay tree with its tangy odor. We loved to run our hands over the madrone trees where the rough bark had peeled away, leaving the satiny smooth, terra-cotta colored trunks. And we used to wonder how the horse chestnut, also known as buckeye, got its names—did someone think that the big, smooth, round, brown nut with a white patch on it resembled an eyeball?

We never did learn the name of the little shrub with the small, waxy white fruits that we passed on our way although I think now it must have been manzanita *(arctostaphylos),* a common native. But we did learn early to recognize the poison oak by the three-leaflet pattern of the leaves and to stay away from it. And we always stopped to examine the solitary pitcher plant that grew by the pathway. It fascinated us because its hollow, tube-like leaves captured and digested insects—a fly-eating plant!

Part way up we reached a small, sparkling waterfall near which ferns grew in profusion, delicate maidenhair drooping alongside pale green, beautifully patterned ones, as well our beloved "stamping ferns" which left a yellow imprint on the skin when you pressed their underside to the back of your hand. Water falling over the twelve-foot bank raised a veil of silver mist in the air. Plants in varying tones and textures, their foliage glossy with wetness, made of the sloping banks a scene of beauty. The waterfall was always the highlight of our walk. Having seen it we were ready at last to start for home.

On our way back we would pick some ferns, a bluebell or two, a bright red Indian paintbrush or perhaps one of the tiny orchids we called "bee flowers." I remember once running across a mother quail and her string of velvety babies. Their mottled gold and brown coloration was such effective camouflage that they soon lost themselves in the dry grass. Though I hunted and hunted I could never find a one.

In these early days of my life a variety of wildlife still roamed the fields and woodlands but, just as we thought trees were there to be cut and wildflowers to be gathered, animals were there to be killed, as predators or as food. Two of my earliest memories are of a dead lynx or bobcat on display in our orchard, presumably having been shot by one of the men in the family, and a lifeless rattlesnake draped over the chicken yard fence. In all the time I was growing up I never saw another rattlesnake, though we occasionally saw garter snakes and large, harmless gopher snakes. I never saw a deer on our property, either, though my brother Tiny used to hunt them on the Las Trampas Range that bordered the ranch. Once in a while he would bag a few quail and bring them home for Mama to bake in the oven. It's hard for me to imagine anything more delicious. Those wild, grain-fed birds had far more flavor than the farm-raised ones now sold in supermarkets.

A few cottontails and some long-eared jackrabbits bounded over the pasture land, with a medium-sized hare or rabbit whose name I don't know. By the time I graduated from high school all were gone. Often, at night, before we fell asleep we could hear the doleful, creepy sound of the coyote's howl. They were survivors and lasted much longer than the rabbits.

Ground squirrels were numerous and voracious, eating a lot of wheat. Sparrow hawks and another, larger hawk—perhaps the red-tailed variety—preyed on her chickens often enough that Ma paid Tiny to shoot them with his .22 rifle. He also set traps for raccoons, ferrets, coyotes and I think even skunks. He skinned them, stretched the tubular skins to dry on a sort of framework and sold them for cash that he saved up to buy a motorcycle with.

We often used to see big black and orange monarch butterflies in the fields. I live in the city now and haven't seen one in years. Cliff swallows gathered mud around the watering trough and carried it up to build their rounded domes under the eaves of the barn. I remember marveling at how clever and knowledgeable they seemed to be at this work. Linnets, sparrows and red-winged blackbirds were plentiful, and now and then a redheaded woodpecker drummed its jackhammer staccato on the old dead trees or crows landed on the walnut tree in the Big Yard. Flickers were only occasional visitors and orioles, too, were scarce although once I did spot one of their skillfully woven sack-nests fastened to the drooping end of a eucalyptus branch where no cat or predator could reach it. It was always thrilling when we saw a dazzling, blue-green humming bird whizzing from the purple lilac to the sweet-smelling honeysuckle in Mama's garden. Although hard to spot in the daytime, at night we would hear the owls' cries—screech owls and barn owls, Tiny said. Blue jays, beautiful as they were, worried Mama with their egg-sucking ways so they were on Tiny's kill-on-sight list. We delighted in this idyllic profusion of birds and wildlife yet we also took it for granted. That's just the way it was. Never did it occur to us that these natural riches would become scarce and some would disappear completely. As I look back on those days from a distance of over eighty years, it seems to me that life on the Home Ranch was not only happy for me and my brothers and sisters but gave security and satisfaction to my parents, too. Those good years must have been compensation to them both for their long, hard early struggles.

Pioneers

IN THE SPRING of 1872, my father, Jose Pires Azevedo, was on his way to the United States from the Azores Islands. He was eighteen years old, illiterate, spoke only Portuguese, and his one resource was some coins his stepmother had sewed into the lining of his coat. He was leaving his home in the village of Beira on the island of São Jorge, where he was born on February 18, 1854. He was headed for New Bedford, Massachusetts and thence to California, which returning Azoreans had described as the land of opportunity. Land was plentiful there, land that would grow almost anything, and the climate was good. In time a man who was ambitious and willing to work could end up with something for his family.

Land to Azoreans was a precious and unobtainable asset. The islands were small and overcrowded, lacking either commerce or industry. On each island all the tillable, level land belonged to one family, which had ruled by gift of the Crown since the islands were settled in the fifteenth century, and which was forbidden by law from selling any part of its holdings. The peasants were relegated to the steep, rocky margins. Although the climate was mild and the volcanic soil was fertile, their plots were as tiny as a suburban back yard and yielded a bare subsistence only with intensive cultivation and good luck. Most people lived in extreme poverty, with no possible way to get ahead. My father said that when he was a boy he was required to get off the road and doff his hat when the *morgado,* the heir to the landed estate, passed by. The institution of *morgadio,* or the single heir, had been legally abolished in the 1830's but in practice the custom survived. Jose learned early that a landowner had the respect of his community.

The sailing ship Galena was packed with 98 Azorean immigrants. What the boy probably hoped would be an exciting adventure turned out to be a trial of fear and hunger that nearly cost him his life. They had not been long at sea before they began to have grave doubts about their captain. Rations of food, always doled out with a miserly hand, shrank every day. They realized that the supply was inadequate for a ship overloaded with passengers. The trip stretched on, weeks after they should have reached port, until it became apparent that the captain had lost his bearings and that they were at the mercy of the sea. The food was almost entirely gone. Their rations went down to one half of a sea biscuit per day. They stopped a passing ship, asked for help, and were given a barrel of salt fish but it was all eaten before Jose got any. Later they stopped a second ship and this time were given a barrel of sea biscuits but these got wet in the transfer by open boat and soon spoiled. Jose reached such a state of desperation that he tried to satisfy his hunger by chewing wood shavings scraped from the door-frame with a knife.

In a storm and with night approaching they spotted an island, possibly Nantucket, and the captain lowered the anchor. It was a sandy bottom. An old sailor told Jose that

Velas, the main town of São Jorge Island, Azores, about 1980. Typical small plots of ground above the town.

the anchor wouldn't hold and that they were in danger of being dashed on the rocks: "We'll drown like rats," he said. He was right, it didn't hold, but luckily the wind dropped and by the next morning they had drifted a long way from the island. They asked a passing ship how far it was to New Bedford and were told they would reach it in two days or less. They reached port on May 23, 1872. The crossing, which was supposed to have taken 18 days, had lasted 56 days.

One passenger died of starvation before they reached port in New Bedford, others were so weak they could barely move and had to be half-carried ashore. The New Bedford newspaper reported that a hearing would be held in New York on the circumstances of the voyage, though I have been unable to find a record of it.

Jose and a friend took a room in a boarding house, then set

out to look for food. Starving men are supposed to eat only a little at a time but they couldn't wait. They found a little bakery and pointed to some doughnuts. I have heard my father tell how a black man, no doubt the first he had ever seen, then set up some boards over a couple of barrels and brought them coffee and all the doughnuts they could eat. He said it was the best food he had ever tasted, though of course they were sick when they got back to the boarding house.

While he waited three weeks for the train to San Francisco, Jose began working for a man who raised vegetables for the market near Providence, Rhode Island. His job was to fertilize a field of corn, using up a big, stinking pile of rotten fish by burying one fish in each hill of sprouting corn. He also had to help his employer gather brush for firewood and he never forgot one incident connected with that job. Having walked up a steep, narrow trail with Jose leading a horse, they collected such a huge pile of wood that he became apprehensive when his boss indicated he should tie it onto the animal so they could leave for home. Without English he didn't know how to express his fear that the giant load would knock the horse off the narrow path and over the cliff into the ravine. He pointed to the horse and spread his arms wide, then at the path and put his hands close together. His boss just laughed and gave the horse a whack with a whip. It dashed off down the path with so much momentum that the load didn't fall off.

At last, Jose was on his way to California aboard the transcontinental train which had only been in existence for about three years. The trip, and the country, must have seemed endless to a young man whose early life had been spent entirely on a small volcanic island in the middle of the Atlantic Ocean.

It was an island only about thirty-three miles long and five miles wide at its maximum dimensions, whose every spare meter was cultivated. I wonder what he thought as he crossed the great plains, mile upon mile upon mile of uncultivated land without a house or a farm in sight, empty except for the rapidly disappearing buffalo and Indians. He told my mother the story of one encounter with Indians. It seems that at some point one of the train's boxcars accidentally got derailed and some of its contents, a shipment of ladies' hats, spilled out on the ground. A band of roving Indians snatched them up, jammed them on their heads and rode off at a gallop, ribbons and feathers floating in the wind. Some disappointed California ladies must have gone without Easter bonnets that year.

On the train he was lucky enough to team up with a young American going west. Although neither spoke the other's language they somehow managed to communicate, as when Jose pointed to himself and said "San Francisco" and the stranger pointed to himself and said the same. The stranger who spoke English looked after Jose in every way he could. Together they scrounged for food whenever the train stopped, for there were no dining cars in those early days. Papa later confided to my mother that he had worried about how fast his money was going for food, but he feared seeming miserly. He was right to worry for when he arrived in San Francisco he had only fifty cents in his pocket, though that would buy a lot more in 1872 than it would today.

Jose had brought with him the address of a San Francisco hotel run by Portuguese people. No doubt his friend helped him locate it, then they parted forever. Jose had never even learned his name. Ever afterward he was sorry that he hadn't for he would have liked to thank him for his helpfulness to a stranger in a strange land.

The following day, Jose made his way to the home of a cousin who lived in the town of Hayward, about thirty miles from San Francisco. As early as 1860 about 600 Azorean immigrants had settled throughout the area east of San Francisco Bay, especially in San Leandro but also in Hayward, Danville, San Ramon and some areas of Oakland. By the early 1870's, when my father arrived, the local Azorean population was growing rapidly and it reached about 5500 immigrant settlers by 1880. Later immigrants were naturally drawn to areas where their own people had gone before and prepared the way. Sometimes there would be friends from home to welcome them and at least there would be countrymen who spoke their language and could give them tips on survival in the new land. I know, for instance, that Papa was acquainted with my mother's parents, who came from his home island and were farming in the Tassajara Valley, southeast of Danville. Certainly there were others as well, and they formed a useful network.

All I know of Pa's brief stay with his cousin is an amusing story of cultural confusion. I don't know whether he had been asked to start the fire in the kitchen wood stove in the morning or whether he just wanted to make himself useful but in any case, going by what he had learned at home in Beira, he carefully built and lit the fire—in the oven instead of in the firebox. At home you built your fire in the brick oven, then as soon as it was good and hot you swept out every vestige of coals and ashes and put your bread in to bake.

But Pa's real life in the new country began when he found work as a shepherd on a ranch in the San Ramon Valley in

Contra Costa County. Mama told me he worked for one pair of overalls, board and room and five dollars a month. Since he spoke no English, the preliminary bargaining had to be accomplished by means of sign language—his prospective employer drew four marks in the dirt and Jose added another to show he wanted five dollars, not four.

Possibly he worked under another name, for some time after his arrival, he anglicized Jose Pires Azevedo to Joe Peters Azevedo and then, finally, to Joe Peters. How this came about I don't know. However, I have read that Azoreans in general attach surprisingly little importance to family names, children taking the last name of either parent and married women sometimes using their maiden names. Perhaps first names are what count in their small villages, often with descriptive adjectives attached for distinguishing one Mary or one John from another. In any case, in this country many Portuguese names were anglicized to related American ones, Perry for Pereira, Oliver for Oliveira, Lawrence for Lourenço and the like. Pires in Portuguese sounds much like Peters and Papa's cousin in Hayward, whose name was Pires, had already anglicized it.

Only a few years later, Joe Peters Azevedo was farming a sizeable property in the Bollinger Canyon, about four miles from the village of San Ramon. My father was remarkably hardworking and frugal, and no doubt he had saved every possible penny from his earnings as he was to do all his life, but it was the 1862 Homestead Act, intended to help settlers in the new western states, that helped him realize his dream of California land in such a short time. That act allowed a citizen, or a man who had declared his intention of becoming one, to claim and take possession of 160 acres of unoccupied public land. All that was required for eventual ownership was that he live on it, cultivate it and improve it for a period of five years.

Accordingly, Pa declared his intent to become a citizen—he was naturalized on May 15, 1884—and filed a claim on a 160 acre plot. I don't know the exact year nor do I know exactly where in the Bollinger Canyon his ranch was located. He raised beef cattle and hogs for sale and apparently thrived.

In 1879, seven years after his arrival in California, he met and married Mary Caton, a young American-born woman of Azorean descent. Papa was then 25, Mary was not yet 15. With her he would establish his first family (my mother was his second wife). In 1880 their first child, Frank, arrived and thereafter children came in rapid succession. A second son, Joe, was born in 1881, followed by their eldest daughter, Mary, in 1883, Annie in 1885 and Louise in 1887. Manuel was born in 1889 and their youngest daughter, Frances, in 1892. At some time during those years, they lost another child who was kicked to death by a horse. I was very young when I overheard someone talking about it but I never learned how or when it happened, or even the age and sex of the child. It was certainly not my father talking, for he almost never mentioned the hardships of his early life.

I wish I knew more about their life in the Canyon, especially their first years there. What little I do know came to me much later in the form of stories or anecdotes from my older half-brothers and sisters, repeated over and over because they were relished by the family, or more indirectly from my own mother. A number of these stories have to do with animals to some degree, for animals were central to farm life. Some may seem callous to modern ears, sensitive as we are to any cruelty to animals. I can only say that while no one in my family was ever deliberately cruel, either to animals or humans, people in general did not empathize with animals in those days the way they do now. They were placed in a different category from humans and seen as meant to serve human purposes. Papa nearly always had a dog and he was certainly fond of his dogs but he viewed them as working partners who helped in rounding up the cattle. They slept in the barn or under the porch but were never allowed in the house. As for the farm cats, they were feral creatures, useful for keeping the mouse population down but thoroughly wild and unpettable. They depended for their food on whatever mice they could catch along with the table scraps that were set out for them and the dog. I doubt that my father ever gave cats a thought.

One story which I heard many times over was the tale of the squatter. Mary Caton discovered one day that a stranger had started to build a cabin on the farthest reaches of their land. As it happened that Papa was away from home at the time, working on a haypress to earn needed cash, she decided she would have to take care of the problem herself. She got Frank and Joe up in the dark of the night, took some axes, and together they tore that cabin down. It never occurred to Mary to appeal to a court of law, if indeed one was readily available, nor would she have had the money for a lawyer anyway. More likely that was the way of the west at the time, a hangover from the spirit of the vigilantes.

Some time after that the would-be squatter showed up at the farmhouse, apparently to make trouble, and Papa recognized him as the man he had rescued with his team not long before when his wagon was stuck in the mire on the steep

Moore Hill. Now as it happened, just as the man arrived the big farm dog was having a fit of some kind and Papa, hoping to cure him, had picked him up by the hind legs and was in the process of dunking him in the watering trough. Seeing this, the man apparently felt he was dealing with a violent character, for he turned around and left, never to be heard from again.

The family house in the Bollinger Canyon was about four miles from the grammar school in San Ramon, not within walking distance. Frank and Joe were expected to squeeze in as much farmwork as possible before they left for school (and more of the same after school as well) so there was always an early-morning rush to get there on time. Joe left first because he had to drive Mary and Annie in the cart. Frank would leave later, on horseback. Many years afterward he told his daughter, Gertrude Rodriguez, that, as he was always pressed for time, he would ride his horse at a full gallop, not breaking stride for a gate that blocked his passage. The force of the impact would pop the wooden latch and the gate would fly open. Hurrying to avoid his teacher's wrath and probably enjoying the drama the boy gave no thought to the need for the gate to remain closed to keep the cattle from wandering.

A favorite story was about the time that one of the older boys accidentally killed a small pig. I have no idea how it happened, although possibly he threw a rock at a recalcitrant one, trying to drive it into its pen. They are notoriously "pig-headed." All I know is that he had a dead pig on his hands and was scared to death to tell Pa. At last he hit upon a solution. There was a wagon in the shed whose long tongue was tied to a rafter to keep it out of everyone's way. He untied the pole and lowered it onto the little pig. The ruse worked. Papa never

The San Ramon Grammar School, about 1894. Louise far left, Annie second from right, Manuel front row, third child from right.

found out. The pig was dead and the pole was on top of him—that was enough. The culprit had used his head to save the seat of his pants.

Another story had to do with a sleeping cow. Frank told it to Gertrude and Gertrude told it to me. Joe, who couldn't have been older than thirteen at the time, was driving Annie to school in the cart. Suddenly, right before them was a sleeping cow, stretched at full length across the road. Joe recklessly urged the horse forward, perhaps in the hope of a little excitement. But the horse was too smart to trample a sleeping cow. He veered to the side in an effort to avoid it, and in the end only one wheel of the cart ran over the cow's hind quarters. No capsized cart, no broken bones, no injured cow —catastrophe averted!

Farm women had a hard life in those early days and Mary Caton was no exception. When she married my father she was little more than a child. Her first baby was born when she was

15, and from that time on she bore child after child while facing all the onerous tasks of keeping up a farm household.

But the family prospered. Like others of his people, Papa was a skillful and diligent farmer. There is a New England saying, "If you want a potato to grow you must speak to it in Portuguese." He enlarged his original homestead of 160 acres by additional purchases of land. First a non-Portuguese neighbor offered to sell an 80-acre piece at a reasonable price. Papa bought it and later bought still more land, bringing his total holdings in Bollinger Canyon up to 539 acres, according to a 1904 assessment. He increased his cattle herd to 25, his hogs to at least 50. And about 1892 he was able to build a new house for the family, a spacious house with a kitchen, dining-room and parlor, five bedrooms and a pantry and basement.

Then, without warning, disaster struck. In 1893, Mary was brought down by pneumonia. Before the discovery of penicillin it was a dread disease, one of the primary killers, and she did not survive. She was only 28. It was a calamity for her family. Papa was devastated, not only by the loss of his wife, but by the enormity of the problems which now confronted him. He alone had full responsibility for seven children ranging from Frank, the eldest at 14, to Frances, the baby, only 2 years old. Yet if he didn't keep up with the farm work they would go hungry.

Ten year old Mary, as the eldest girl, was taken out of school to manage the household and care for the younger children. That was the end of her education and her childhood. As an adult, Mary would be high-spirited, energetic and conscientious, so she would probably have been equal to the task if she had been a few years older, but it was too much for her at that tender age. Papa probably helped as much as possible but he couldn't spare much time from his farm work and anyway he knew next to nothing of what to him had always been women's work.

I don't know why my father didn't hire a housekeeper to spare Mary. He had just bought a house and may have been short of cash. Certainly he would never have considered taking a loan or mortgaging the house, since all his life he paid cash for everything, even his properties. Still, I doubt that was the reason. A man from the old country would have had a different outlook on such things. The women in the family did the housework. The idea of hiring outside help would be foreign to him. Furthermore, all the women in Papa's Azorean family and probably most of the men were illiterate. From his point of view, Mary had had a lot of schooling already.

Food was the first necessity. Flour, sugar, coffee and beans were bought in Danville, in large quantities to save trips to town. But bread was a major problem. It was the staple food and one the children needed for school lunches. It had to be made at home twice a week as the nearest bakery was 16 miles away in Hayward. I never heard how they managed that. I don't see how Mary could have done it—possibly Papa paid some neighbor woman to make extra for his family. Mary probably learned soon enough how to fry meat and boil ordinary vegetables like potatoes, corn, string beans, peas and cabbage but dry beans, another staple, were a different matter. How could she have known that they needed long cooking, especially if they were not presoaked? Years later her brothers still teased her about her "bullet beans." For breakfast there would have been homemade bacon which had to be sliced by hand and then parboiled to remove excess salt before it could be fried. Huge plattersful of fried eggs would be easy after that. The laundry would have been a second major problem. It all had to be done by hand, after heating the water, and it is heavy work to get farm clothes clean by scrubbing on a washboard.

The younger children must have been left largely to their own devices for how could Mary have found time to watch them? Of course, left unsupervised, they got into mischief and their innocent play could even be dangerous. A neighbor, passing by the place one day and seeing one of the children carrying a large suitcase, insisted on opening it up when he saw movement indicating something inside. He was right. It was two-year-old Frances! No doubt because of that scare, Frances was sent to live with her maternal grandmother, who lived with an unmarried, crippled daughter on the outskirts of Hayward. Mrs. Caton took care of Frances for three years until Papa remarried. Years later when Mrs. Caton was very old and poor, Papa arranged with a local grocer to give her whatever food she needed and charge it to him. I suppose he would have wanted to take care of her in any case but he never forgot the help she had given him when he needed it so badly.

If a kid needed shoes, Papa would have had to make the hour and a half trip by horse and cart to Hayward. Dresses and children's shirts were usually made at home in those days. Mary didn't sew and as they were all growing rapidly, the children's clothing went to near-rags. I know this because my mother told me that when in 1897 she married Papa and took charge of his family she found them almost destitute of clothing, the girls having only one dress apiece. Mama had her work cut out for her.

Peters Family Tree

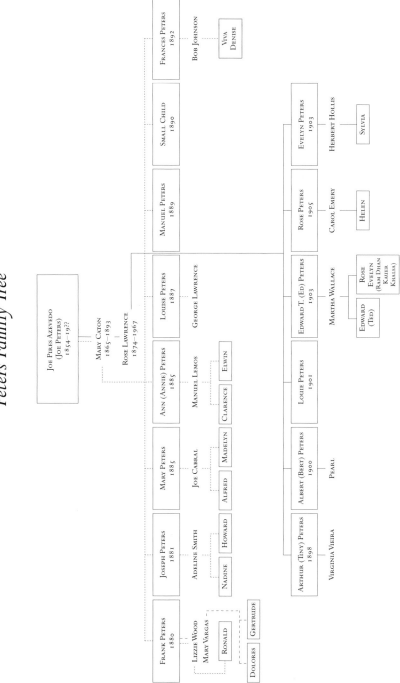

Mama's Early Life

MY MOTHER, Rose Lawrence, was 23 in 1897 when she married my father, shared in the running of his large farm and took over the care of his seven children. His oldest son, Frank, about 17, was out of school but still lived at home and worked on the ranch so he, too, had to be fed and his clothes washed. One would think all this would be a daunting undertaking for such a young woman, especially one who had been lame from birth (one hip socket was misplaced so that her right leg was a couple of inches shorter than the other and she had to wear a built-up shoe). However, when she was about ninety years old, telling me about her youth, my mother said that she considered her married life easy when compared to all she had had to do at home.

Her mother, my grandmother, was born Maria Souza Faustinho Amaral in my father's home village of Beira on the island of São Jorge. She emigrated to the United States at the age of 23 in about 1865, so she was approximately seven years older than my father and must have known him—it was and still is a very small place. She was almost certainly illiterate, for illiteracy was common among Azorean men and nearly universal among poor Azorean women. Although Maria had no friends or relations in New York City and spoke no English, for two years she had to stay on there to earn the fare to California where she had cousins. Possibly she also had to repay her ship's passage, for I recently heard that captains would bring penniless people over and place them in jobs where they would work to repay their fare and the captain's commission. Azoreans were in demand because they were hard workers and expected little in the way of wages. She did housework for about a year while she learned a little English, then made buttonholes in a men's suit factory.

About 1867 my grandmother could finally afford to make the trip west. Although I never heard anything about it, she must either have sailed around the Horn or come overland, partly by wagon train, since the transcontinental railroad wasn't yet complete. She found a job doing housework for a wealthy family in Danville. After that she worked for Charlie Wood on a farm near Danville. The Woods milked about 20 cows and made butter to sell. Grandma used to say that the cows were milked outside in the rain in a corral that was knee deep in mud, so it may be that she had to help with the milking. The milk was poured into milk pans in the milk room and the cream skimmed off by hand with a skimmer (like a tin saucer with a handle and holes in it), then churned into butter in a wooden churn.

My grandmother worked for about three years in Danville. She met my grandfather, Manuel Laurence, according to my cousin Rose Ferreira, when he came to work as a hired hand on the Wood farm in 1869. His name was probably anglicized from the Portuguese Laurenço; it was later spelled "Lawrence." Grandpa was Azorean, too, and had emigrated at about the same time that she did, probably from the same island though I don't know if he came from the same village. He must have been literate since the family story was that he had studied to be a priest but changed his mind and came to California. When they married in 1870, Maria (now Mary) was 28 and Manuel was 27.

She had amassed $400 in savings, a goodly sum in those days. My grandfather, however, was nearly penniless. He had worked in the Nevada silver mines but apparently spent his money as fast as he made it because, like many another, he thought there would be no end to the bonanza. Luckily, my grandmother's money was enough to buy a team of good horses, with a sizeable amount left over. Having no land, they decided to sharecrop on a section of the Dougherty Ranch, a 5000 acre spread in Alameda and Contra Costa Counties near Dublin. Its acreage was subdivided into twelve 400-acre plots. These were parceled out to sharecroppers who kept three-fourths of the crop for themselves, the owner getting the other fourth. It was about six miles to the nearest store in Danville and an equal distance to the town of Pleasanton. Mary and Manuel were able to buy seed and a few basic necessities on credit, pledging to pay for these items when the crops were sold. Fortunately, a five-room house with a large kitchen, parlor and three bedrooms came with the farm at no extra rent.

They had been in the house for barely a week and were desperate with worry as to how they could manage to live until the first crop was harvested when one morning they saw the figure of a man trudging over the dirt road that led across their bare fields to the house on the hill. They could not imagine who could be coming to visit them but as he came nearer they

Marriage photo of Manuel Lawrence and Mary Souza Amaral, the author's maternal grandparents, 1870.

saw that it was Joe Souza (no relation to Grandma), whom they had known back in the old country. He had heard via the Azorean grapevine that they were living there and he was looking for work. Luck was with them. Joe had already worked in the United States for wages for a few years and had saved a little nest egg. My grandparents persuaded him to go into partnership with them. They were then able to buy a few minimal essentials like a plow, harrow, wagon, a setting hen, a couple of pigs, a cow and the barest of furnishings for the house. A friend from the old country made Grandma a loom on which she wove squares for a rug. She must have done the cooking for both men.

The partnership lasted for four years, then Grandpa farmed for himself for four more years until he could buy a farm of 160 acres for $4000. This farm was about three miles from the first and, like it, was about six miles from Danville. There were already seven children in the family, including my mother, then called Rosa, who was about five years old. She was born on August 23, 1874, the year her future husband homesteaded in the Bollinger Canyon. In addition to his own farm, every other year my grandfather farmed on shares an additional two hundred acres belonging to a neighbor. The neighbor was raising horses and each year my grandfather would buy some colts from him, break them, and use them to plant and harvest his crop. When this was done he would sell the trained horses at a profit.

The children went to the Sycamore School when they could. It was too far to walk so they rode two to a horse or in a cart when there were four of them. However, their education was sketchy. The roads were so bad during the winter months that the horses were knee deep in mud, so they stayed at home from December through February and whenever it looked like rain. Miss Charlotte E. Wood taught about 17 pupils in the

Sycamore School, 1914. Miss Charlotte E.Wood with pupils.

tiny, one-room school. Most of the children in the family went to the fifth or sixth grade. Only George, the youngest, finished grammar school. Rosa stayed on through most of the seventh grade. Then, on March 18, 1886, her father died suddenly and she had to quit school because she was needed at home.

The family story was that Manuel had been working in the fields in spite of a bad cold and came home feeling very ill. Although overheated, he drank some cool wine from the cellar, was overcome by chills and took to his bed. He died of double pneumonia nine days later, even though the country doctor stayed by his bed for two entire days in an effort to save his life. At 44 years old, after 16 years of marriage, Grandma Mary was left alone with a farm to manage and twelve children to bring up: Mary, 14; Annie, 13; Luisa, 12; Rosa (my mother),

Lawrence children in the Sycamore School, about 1886. First row from left: Will, George, Manuel. Second row: Belle fifth from left; Mariana sixth from left. Standing: Rose third from left; Nellie sixth from right; Josie second from right.

11; Bill, 10; Nellie, 8; Josie, 7; the twins Isabel and Manuel, 6; Mariana, 5; Joe, 3; and George, 2. (She had also miscarried one child.)

What resources there were were soon dissipated. Prices had been so low that crops from previous years were stored in a warehouse at Pleasanton in hopes of better prices later. An appointed administrator made trips here and there trying to sell them, charging for his time and expenses. Soon, both crops and money were gone (some insurance money had also dwindled). Despairing from the loss of her husband, Grandma now believed—rightly or wrongly—that she had received too little money and had been swindled. My mother told me that she couldn't seem to get herself together after Grandpa died, just sat around on a chair and got "real crabby" with the kids.

Nowadays we would say she suffered a profound depression. Her children had to manage on their own.

The boys were too young to be of any significant help so Grandma's cousin, Tony Foster (anglicized from Faustinho), came to run the farm. He put in the crops and somehow they managed to survive—there was no welfare in those days. The older girls, including Mama, took over care of the young ones, helped with the farm work and did all the food preparation, cooking, washing and cleaning. She told me that her life was very hard, and especially so after her older sisters married and left the ranch, leaving her to cope essentially by herself.

Eventually, they milked seven cows, Mama milking three of them. Butter and eggs were traded at the store every week for flour and those few essentials that could not be produced on the farm—pink beans, salt, sugar and coffee—so little butter and few eggs were left over for their own use. Bread had to be baked about three times a week. If it ran short they would fill in with biscuits or cornbread. Three or four pigs were killed each year, to be salted or made into bacon or Portuguese garlic sausage *(linguiça)* or blood sausage *(morcela)*. Once a year they made a trip to Martinez to bring home a load of salmon —perhaps fifteen fish weighing 15 to 28 pounds each, at fifty cents apiece, enough to make two barrels of salt fish. They sliced them, covered them with coarse salt and weighted them down so that they formed their own brine and kept indefinitely. They made their own cheese, clabbering the milk by adding rennet, derived from the stomach of a calf or a wild rabbit and bought at a butcher shop. They also made cottage cheese which was used the year round.

Corn, kale, turnips, cabbages, peas, beets, onions, pump-

Mary Lawrence seated, with 10 of her 12 children at home in Tassajara, about 1894.
From left: Mariana, Will, Manuel, Joe, George, Nellie, Annie, Josie, Rose, Belle.

kins and potatoes were planted in the spring and the wild mustard greens that grew in the fields added variety to their diet. They made the pumpkins into pies and put up apples, plums, peaches, pears and apricots from their home orchard in tin cans sealed with melted rosin. Apples, plums and apricots were dried in the sun, with the smaller children cutting and spreading the fruit. They learned young to work hard.

Mama took it on herself to do much of the cooking. Breakfasts consisted usually of sourdough pancakes, leavened by a yeast starter kept in a fruit jar, bacon and coffee. In addition there were two big meals a day. The dinner at mid-day centered around beef in summer and pork preserved by salting in winter, together with potatoes and beans, greens or other vegetables, and a dessert of canned fruit. The evening meal might be of salmon, parboiled to remove excess salt, beans or hash, again with vegetables and fruit or rice pudding.

She often served *caldo verde,* the staple soup of the Azorean peasant, made of greens cooked with onions, potatoes and a little lard. Occasionally she made macaroni, cooked with onions and tomatoes or in a meat soup. Homemade cheese was a staple. Wine was served occasionally.

With all this responsibility and stuck out there on the farm as she was, Rose (her Americanized name) had a problem. How could she find someone she would want to marry? Her only social life was right at home where about once a week on Sunday afternoon or evening there was dancing to the music of the violin and banjo, played by Nellie's and Annie's husbands. The dancers were the eight young women of the family, the two older boys and four to seven farm workers from local ranches. They danced the *chamarita* and other Portuguese dances as well as the waltz, schottische, Virginia reel and polka—no square dancing.

Rose's lameness had probably spoiled some of her chances; at twenty-three, she was past the prime marriage age and on her way to spinsterhood. So when Joe Peters Azevedo appeared at the ranch looking for a wife (he may have approached her mother first, or had someone else speak in his favor), although she didn't know him personally she was favorably inclined. He was 20 years older than she was but he was strong and healthy, and he was known to be hardworking and reliable, a good farmer. He already owned a sizeable property, and the year before his first wife died he had built a new house for his family—a big, comfortable house compared to the small, overcrowded one she knew at home. As for Joe, he was desperate for help at home and probably lonely. It must have been a short courtship, probably no more than two or three

Marriage photo of Joe Peters and Rose Lawrence, 1897.

visits where they sat on the porch and talked, for he couldn't have spared much time away from home. It appears to have been a marriage of convenience, though Mama did tell me she thought he was good-looking. Together they formed a working partnership that seemed to have developed over the years into genuine affection.

Mama brought only workaday clothes to her marriage in 1897, but she splurged a little on her wedding outfit. She hired a dressmaker to design and make for her a more elaborate dress in the tight-waisted, mutton-sleeved fashion of the day. My parents took a trip by train to Sacramento for their honeymoon. Mama was dressed up for the occasion in a big hat with a feather on it—I envision it as one of the ostrich plumes that were so popular at the time. Whatever it was, the tip of it kept striking Papa's face whenever she turned her head. My brother Frank said that he didn't complain, but after a time just quietly broke off the tip of the feather. Some people might find such an action surprising, especially on a honeymoon, but it

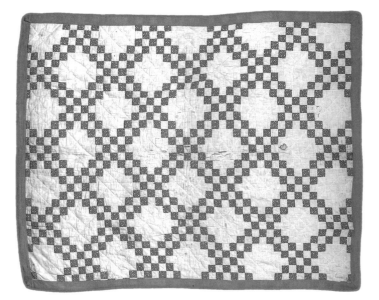

Quilt in the Double Irish Chain pattern, red and white cotton, made by Rose Lawrence before 1897.

doesn't surprise me. Papa had a quirky, almost perverse sense of humor, and it reflected his disdain for what he considered women's foolish acceptance of lamebrain fashions.

Rose brought no money to the marriage, no hope chest filled with linens, no trousseau of fine clothing. The one household item she owned was her patchwork quilt. Sewn by hand in an intricate pattern of red and white squares, it was ample proof of her skill with a needle, and more than a hundred years later it is still treasured by the family. But she was brought up in a household almost identical to the one she was to manage, she had acquired every skill she needed to run a house, bring up children, and contribute to the running of a farm, and she would work with all her strength for her family.

Mama took charge immediately. She saw what needed to be done and then did it. I quote from the account she wrote out for me when she was ninety:

> We needed spending money. So I decided we milk cows and sell butter. For the first butter that I sold I got $11.50. I drove to Hayward in the cart and bought 20 yards of material for $1.00 at five cents a yard, plus cotton stuffing to make quilts. Then I bought 30 yards of calico at ten cents a yard to make dresses for the girls. [I bought] material for shirts, flannel for nightgowns, muslin for underwear, and socks and stockings. I drove home with the cart piled full. Just before I came, water was piped from the spring into the kitchen and onto the back porch. We had a long zinc bathtub. Water was warmed on the

stove and poured into it. We had bare wood floors but later we had matting in the bedrooms and a rug in the living room. We bought furniture for the parlor and a couch and six extra chairs for the dining room. There was a new wood stove. The only other heat was the fireplace in the dining-room. I bought a bolt of curtain yardage and made curtains for the entire house.

At first she sold butter—a lot of it, to judge by the huge wooden churn that sat empty in our backyard for many years. It was a wooden box about 4½ feet square mounted on a special stand, with a stout wooden handle for turning all that heavy cream and a clamp-down lid to prevent leakage. Later, however, she learned it was more profitable just to sell the cream to a dairy.

Five-year-old Frances was brought home from her grandmother's. Mary was freed from most of her heavy responsibilities. And before long more children began to arrive, first Tiny, then four more of us of the second family, giving Papa 12 living children in all. With my mother's thrift and hard work added to my father's, the family continued to prosper—more milk cows, more beef cattle were raised. Then in 1906, when I was less than a year old, Papa sold the place in Bollinger Canyon and bought the George Wood ranch in San Ramon, a choice property of 256 acres. I mention Papa only because, while Mama might give advice and must have been indispensible for handling contracts since he couldn't read, he always had the final say on any business transactions and in fact on all

The Peters House in Bollinger Canyon, about 1900. From left: farm hand (?), Joe Peters holding Tiny, Frances, Rose Peters holding Bert, Frank (?), Joe, Jr.

matters except those relating to food, clothing, household furnishings and routine care of children—Mama's domain. The ranch was on the main road through the San Ramon Valley, a good gravel road, so the new place was less isolated than the old one. It was only a scant mile from the San Ramon School we all attended, one after the other, and four miles from Danville in the other direction. Besides, the land wasn't so steep and the soil was better.

But Papa wanted still more land. Within two or three years he decided to buy the 216-acre Butcher ranch, which Mama said cost him $10,000. That was a lot of money in the years just before 1910. His final purchase, soon thereafter, was the

Palmer ranch, 168 acres adjoining the Butcher ranch, for which he paid $14,200. The total area of all his holdings was now 640 acres. He must have taken great pride in all that he had achieved since his penniless arrival from the Azores. With his wives' invaluable help, he had made of himself a man of property, a respected member of the community who need not be subservient to anyone.

Just before the move to their new home in San Ramon, the great San Francisco earthquake struck on April 18, 1906, shaking the Canyon house so hard that the chimney collapsed, and the contents of the big metal milk tank sloshed out onto the ground. I was six months old. My memories begin a few years later, on the new ranch.

My Family

A TRAVELING PHOTOGRAPHER once took a picture of
Ed, Mama, me, Evelyn, Papa and Frances on our front porch.
I still have that picture and I treasure it. It is the only one from
my youth that shows most of my immediate family together
(unfortunately, Tiny and Bert were off somewhere). All of us
are just standing there staring at the camera except Mama and
Frances, who look lost in their own thoughts. Evelyn is wearing her customary shy and downcast expression. Of course we
had to stand very still for the long exposure, but anyway, Pa
didn't like us to smile broadly; he thought it unseemly. "Don't
show your teeth," he used to say. We are dressed just as we happened to be at the time, Ev and me with our droopy black
stockings, Ev's little drawers peeking out, and me with the
boy's boots I hated, handed down from my brother Ed because
they happened to fit me and were in too good a condition to
waste.

We children saw Papa as the boss, a powerful, authoritar-
ian figure. That wasn't all bad. With Pa in charge, we felt
secure: everything was taken care of so we had nothing to
worry about. Certainly it was he who set the tone and pace of
living in our family. He kept us kids in line, and there was no

On the front steps of the farmhouse, about 1912. Left to right: Ed, Rose Lawrence Peters, Rose, Evelyn, Joe Peters, Frances.

doubt about what was expected of us. Even obstreperous Tiny tried to avoid any confrontation with him. Most parents in those days believed it was their duty to control their children by physical punishment. "Spare the rod and spoil the child," was the common saying. However, Papa had such a loud, gruff voice and stern manner that it wasn't necessary for him to hit us. His was a voice that demanded—and got—instant obedience.

Only once do I remember Papa striking any of us and then, unsurprisingly, it was Tiny who was beaten. Tiny loved guns and had two of them. First he bought a BB gun but graduated before long to a .22. Mama was happy to have him shoot the hawks that preyed on her chickens. All went well for a while and then came near-disaster. One day he stood in the orchard and shot at a hawk that was perched on a fencepost near the road. At that precise moment a local Japanese farmer on a bicycle shot out from behind a bank at the side of the road and Tiny's bullet took a nick out of one of his ears. To ease the man's understandable wrath, Papa gave him a twenty dollar gold piece. Then he dealt with Tiny. I happened to be in the orchard at the time and saw Tiny down on the ground with Pa standing over him, beating him with a short piece of garden hose. I was so frightened I could hardly bear it. Later I heard that when the local Japanese farmers would see Tiny passing by, they'd put their heads together and whisper. Who could blame them? And yet I know that Tiny meant no harm

I don't remember our mother ever spanking me. It's true that if one of us kids annoyed her when she was sewing we might get a sharp rap on the head with her thimble and we probably did get spanked occasionally when we were little. Tiny, however, was always in trouble. Once when Mama was about ninety she told me, laughing, about the time when Tiny and Bert had been involved in some escapade and she sent each of them out to cut a switch for her to use on the other's legs. Dear easy-going, good-natured Bert came back with a fragile twig that would hardly have hurt a fly. Ma found this so funny she couldn't go on with the punishment and sixty years later she enjoyed retelling the story.

Mama's temperament was not explosive like Papa's and while she, too, expected obedience she was less rigid, more amenable to concessions. If she asked you to fill the wood box, for instance, and you wanted a moment to finish whatever it was you were doing, you could call "Just a minute," and not be asking for trouble. Not so with Pa.

He was a hard man, but not a hard-hearted one. Once, for

instance, he traveled a long distance by train to testify as a character witness for a man he knew who had got into some kind of serious trouble. More than once he hitched up his team to haul a traveler's car out of the mud, and of course to take any payment was unthinkable. Moreover he never said no to a tramp who wanted to sleep in the barn, though he first made him turn out his pockets to show that he had no matches. Even a spark in a horse barn full of hay can spell disaster.

In fact, both my parents were generous with others in need. Hoboes would often stop at the farmhouse and ask for something to eat. Neither my father, who had known what it is to be hungry, nor my mother, with her generous heart, ever wanted to refuse food to anyone. Mama would make up a plate of whatever we had had for lunch, usually meat, potatoes, beans and a vegetable, for them to eat outside on the back porch. Then there was the time a Japanese farmer rented a plot of land on our Palmer ranch flats to plant tomatoes. Though it wasn't part of the bargain Pa saw the need and without being asked hauled over a large tank of water to help the man get his plants started. Another Japanese farmer, a tenant on the Meese ranch, came one day to ask if he could buy milk for his baby. He was told to bring a pail every day and get as much as he needed free of charge. Later he and his wife came over with a thank you gift of a linen tablecloth. Mama and Papa, thinking they had done only a small favor, respected their scrupulousness but said they "wished they hadn't done it."

Once a couple's automobile broke down near our house. Cars were few and far between in those days and probably less reliable than now. Although the people were total strangers, my parents invited them in, gave them supper and a bed for the night, then breakfast in the morning. Soon after they left, a crate of oranges arrived in the mail together with a big supply of raisins of the type still clinging to the stems. How we children enjoyed them! We had never seen so many before. Once in a while Mama bought a few raisins for cooking and Ed, Ev and I would manage to wheedle a few out of her—she'd pour maybe eight or so into each outstretched hand and we'd eat the cherished morsels slowly so they'd last longer. Nowadays I can eat as many as I like on my oatmeal for breakfast, but they don't taste half as good as they used to.

Papa had a reputation as an honest man, a man who paid his debts, cheated no one and whose word was good. Because he had the respect of the community, about 1921, he was elected to the San Ramon school board together with our schoolmate Kenneth Fry's mother. They had the responsibility for deciding what was needed and how to spend the tax money. Since Papa was always honest in his business dealings, he expected others to be the same. A family story was that once he sold some steers to a cattle buyer, and when they were being weighed he noticed that the scales had been set in the buyer's favor. He drove all the cattle off the big platform scales and refused to complete the transaction until a correction was made. He may have been an illiterate foreigner but he was nobody's fool.

Although he couldn't work them out on paper, Pa had some mysterious way of figuring out a lot of things in his head—for example, if a cattle buyer offered a given price per pound he could somehow arrive at a rough estimate of what he'd get for the entire herd. Of course he had the advantage of Ma's help when he needed it. Because she could read and write

English she would make out the orders from the Sears and Roebuck catalog, check bills for accuracy, write receipts, and keep necessary records. She also wrote the checks although Papa eventually learned to write his own signature in big, clumsy, sprawly letters so he didn't have to sign with an x. Nobody who saw that signature once could ever mistake it for another's.

Mama was extremely thrifty but she wasn't stingy. She had no fancy dishes, no jewelry, and very few clothes. She had the same best dress for years, in a dark color with a small print on a matte fabric, probably silk crepe or fine wool. She never complained yet I believe she sometimes had a yearning for small luxuries. One of the things Ev and I found in her trunk was what she called her "mink." It was an elaborate neck piece concocted of a series of about six mink pelts. The bodies went over her shoulders and the heads, fitted with tiny artificial eyes, lined up in a row across her bosom, the tails hanging down beneath them. I never saw her wear it, even to church. I think it probable that her step-daughter Louise, noted for her "truth-telling," informed her it was out of fashion.

Despite her thriftiness, when Mama really wanted something she usually managed to get it. For as long as I could remember we kept a surrey with a fringe on top in the wagon shed, a fancy item that must have been her doing. We almost never used it, though. Perhaps it was outmoded by then. The carpets and parlor furniture were her idea, too, as well as the telephone and the flush toilet—even, about 1921, a Buick automobile. I think that without her Papa would never have bought anything not directly connected to farm work or absolutely indispensable to living, like basic food, clothing, and furniture.

I marvel now at Mama's admirable adaptation to a difficult life and the hard work and devotion that she lavished on her family. I fully appreciate the remarkable woman my mother was; the popular sport of mom-bashing never appealed to me. We weren't much for hugs and kisses in our family yet despite all the demands on her time and attention, Mama somehow found time to do little things that showed she loved us. In cold weather she would put warm irons into our beds to make us comfortable or warm a sheet to wrap us up in after a bath. Anytime we happened to be around when the bread dough was risen and ready, Ma would pull and shape small pieces of dough and make us some fritters by frying them in hot fat and sprinkling them with sugar. These tasted as good to us as the homemade doughnuts she often made.

Once, probably before I was old enough for school, Ed and I were playing around the sewing machine while Mama sewed. Ed asked if he could sew something, too. She promptly cut out for him a teddy bear's coat with set-in sleeves, then showed him how to put it together. It is funny now to think of a future Brigadier General of the U.S. Marines sewing doll clothes, but it never seemed to enter Mama's mind that sewing might be considered a sissy thing for a boy to do.

I, being two years younger, was greatly impressed that Ed could make anything so marvelous as that little coat, and I immediately determined to learn to sew for myself. Mama taught me to sew, first by hand and then on the machine, while I was still in grammar school. I took to it right away because, like Ed, I have always loved to work with my hands. After I learned to sew, various sewing chores fell to me—mending socks, for example. I remember once trying to put a patch on the knee of Pa's pants while he still had them on. Some of my stitches went all the way through and caught in his long underdrawers so I had to undo the whole job. Papa found it all very amusing.

Although it was never the custom to pay any attention to birthdays in our family, I remember that kind Frances once broke the rule and made Ev and me our own birthday cake— our birthdays were just a day apart. It was decorated with walnut halves on top. We seldom had cakes and that was a very special one.

As a single young woman, Frances was naturally more concerned with appearance than the rest of us. I used to admire her as I watched her dress in her best clothes for church. Like everyone in those days, she wore high shoes, fashionable brown leather ones with matching cloth tops. They were laced up instead of buttoned as was usual and I thought them very elegant. To achieve the desired slender waist, she wore a special, shaped corset that came down over the hips, reached up under the breasts and was pulled tight with laces in the back. I used to help her by pulling on the laces. Mama wore corsets too, as did all women then, but she didn't lace hers so tightly because tight-lacing interfered with work. Brassieres had not yet been invented. A little knit vest was worn under the corset, and over it an unshaped corset cover reached from the waist to a round, lace-decorated neck. Frances had a long-sleeved, high-necked, tight-waisted blue velvet dress that I especially loved. It was probably made by Mrs. Reed, a dressmaker in Danville who Mama sometimes hired to make our best clothes. Readymade dresses were not easily available then. Most women sewed their own.

What I remember best about our cousin John Soares was hearing Frances try to teach him to read English from a primer she had. "The blue beard is in the trrrree. He sing for you and me," he would say. Child that I was, I puzzled over what he meant by "the blue beard." I remember, too, that Mama once had him bob my hair for me. She was convinced that cutting it would make it come in stronger and thicker and better. Masses of long hair were much prized in those days and she thought mine was too thin. Big colored paper hair bows in a special metal clasp were all the fashion then and I happily wore one on my newly bobbed hair.

We kids of the second family were together a great deal. Tiny, the oldest, had boundless energy and was always inventing something or up to something. He had dropped out of high school after a short time and worked for Papa on the ranch, but somehow he found time for all kinds of other activities. He was great fun but he got into a lot of trouble, too. Papa used to say that he was *"atrevido."* I always assumed that meant "bad" or "mischievous" until I studied Spanish and learned that it meant "bold" or "daring."

Once Tiny came up with what he no doubt thought was an ingenious proposal for protecting the house from burglars: he would set up a gun over the doorway in such a way that opening the door would pull the trigger. Of course my parents thought it preposterous. We felt so safe in our home that we never even locked the doors and anyway, how could the gun tell who was friend or foe?

Another time, when Tiny was in his late teens, Pa gave him some dynamite to split a log with. He was supposed to use half a stick but with Tiny if some was good, more was better. He

Freshman class at San Ramon Valley Union High School, about 1912. Tiny Peters seated right.

used a whole stick and half the big log was blown up against the house near the back bedroom window. It smashed the siding, knocked down a lot of plaster, pushed the bureau way out from the wall, and scared Mama out of her wits.

Bert was the unobtrusive one. Steady and deliberate in his work, quiet in his manner, he never caused his parents or teachers any problems. Bert hated to call attention to himself while Tiny—quick and high-spirited, the jokester in the crowd—enjoyed being the center of attention and usually was. Bert never went to high school, which was not yet compulsory, but continued to help Pa with the farm work for several years and became especially skilled at carpentry. He liked to spend his Sundays off hanging out with friends at Hurst's General

Hurst's General Store and San Ramon Post Office, before 1924.

Store in San Ramon, swapping tidbits of local news or playing horseshoes in the schoolyard. I don't know all the rules of this game but it involved driving an iron stake into the ground and tossing horseshoes at it, underhand, in the hopes of getting a "ringer" with the horseshoe surrounding the stake, or at least a "leaner." The fact that horseshoes were so readily available encouraged this sport.

As for Ed, he had a pleasant, even disposition, was less introverted than Bert but not so volatile as Tiny and universally well-liked. As a growing boy with an insatiable appetite, Ed could never get enough of Mama's homemade bread, especially hot out of the oven and dripping with butter. He had a habit of dashing full speed into the kitchen after school, yelling, "Ma!

I'm famished!" Then he would cut two or three big slabs from the loaf and devour them in no time.

Ed sometimes joined in Ev's and my games and we got along very well. Only once do I remember quarreling with him, when he and I got into a fight over a library book. A tiny public library had opened up in Danville and I had taken out a book. I was called away from it to some small job and when I came back Ed was reading it and refused to give it back. When I tried to snatch it away from him the covers came off. I remember I felt quite self-righteous about my innocence and Ed's guilt, but the sad part of this story was that after that Mama wouldn't let us take out any more books.

When our schoolmate Kenneth Fry came by to visit, he would stand outside by the gate and call Ed by whistling for him. Amused by this, Papa always referred to Kenneth as *"o melro"* ("the bird"—actually "the blackbird" but Pa called all songbirds by that name). Our brothers could go off to meet their friends because after a certain age they were allowed to come and go as they pleased so long as their work was done. But except at school we girls had almost no contact with children outside the family because Papa thought girls should be at home where they could be watched over, not running around as the boys did.

In these attitudes, he was only reflecting what he had been taught. Just five years before Papa left the islands, Mark Twain visited them and in *The Innocents Abroad* he described the *capote,* a ridiculous, yard-deep hood, attached to a cape, that Azorean women then wore for modesty in public ("It fits like a circus tent," he said, "and a woman's head is hidden away in it like the man who prompts the singers from his tin shed in the stage of

Kenneth Fry and Eddie Peters, 1917.

an opera.") The capote was almost extinct by the 1940's but as late as twenty-five years ago unmarried Azorean women, whatever their age, were expected to stay within the house and yard unless accompanied by a male relative. It took the fall of the Salazar dictatorship, increasing contact with the European community, and the arrival of television to loosen the restrictions on women.

The first dress I ever made, in the seventh or eighth grade, was of cotton flannelette in thin vertical stripes of medium and dark gray, with a gathered skirt, high neck and long sleeves. I remember how pleased I was when my father praised me for doing a very good job, but I think now his approval was as much for the modest design and color as for my sewing skills.

We just had to conform as best we could to Papa's old-country ways. I recall that he once disapproved of some v-necked dresses that Mama made for Ev and me, and it wasn't that they were in any way immodest for my mother was a very proper woman. On such occasions Mama usually said nothing but went ahead and did as she saw fit. The closest to a quarrel I ever heard between them was once when he said to her, annoyed when she did something after he had expressed disapproval, *"Tu sempre es temosa."* ("You certainly are stubborn.")

In all my life I never heard either of my parents address or even refer to each other by their first names. If talking with outsiders it would be "my husband" or "my wife." If they were talking to us, it was always "Pa says…" or "Ask Ma." The children of the first family referred to Mama as "the old lady" and my father also used that phrase when talking to them about her, though who started it I don't know, nor do I know if it had the same disrespectful sound to them that it has now. But I do remember that Frances told me regretfully, much later, that she and her brothers and sisters had kept their distance because their maternal grandmother was always reminding them that Mama wasn't their real mother.

My niece Dolores told me that her father, my oldest brother Frank, never addressed or spoke of any of his children by name, either. Ronald was "Boy" or "the kid," Dolores was "Girl" and Gertrude was "Baby." I don't know why this was so, but I have since known country people from Italy who have similar customs. Is it a sort of modesty, shielding a private relationship? Or could it be the result of some superstition I wasn't told about?

When we were growing up, Evelyn and I spent all our

time together. We had no next-door neighbors to play with and almost always came right home from school, even when we reached high school, so we were isolated on the farm. Like all kids we sometimes quarreled but we had good times and laughed a lot. Mama always said Evelyn was "particular," meaning she liked her clothes and everything else just so. Except for Tiny we were all shy but Ev was probably the most timid of us all. She was Papa's pet and, as the youngest child, all his life he called her "*Bebê.*" Of course this may also have been because for some regrettable reason she was given an English name he found impossible to pronounce.

Still, she was once on the receiving end of Papa's wrath. She told me that she found a rotten egg laid by some free-roaming chicken in a shed near the pigpen. (You can tell an egg is rotten if you hear its contents thud against the shell when you shake it.) She was standing out in the Big Yard wondering how to get rid of it and Papa was standing a few feet away. Suddenly she wound up her arm like a pitcher about to deliver a fast ball—a zinger, we called them in our Big Yard ball games—and let fly with the egg, aiming into the field. But the crazy thing—it must have been to blame—flew off at an angle and went splat against the blade of a shovel Papa was holding. What a stink! He exploded in a stream of rapid Portuguese, unintelligible to her for the most part but beginning with "*O rapariga do diabo!*," an expression we had heard before when he was angry that meant "O child of the devil!" though I suppose he didn't realize he was thereby demonizing himself. Ev was terrified at first but Papa soon cooled down, realizing that it was an accident, and no carnage resulted. Probably he even saw the humor of the situation.

Holidays were for family. Easter was the least special one —we went to church as usual and bought no fancy clothes, though once we did have a special Easter bread with boiled eggs inside. Thanksgiving and Christmas were the important family feast times. It was then we caught up with our older brothers and sisters, for everyone in the family was invited. Since Papa's living children with their spouses and children then totaled 26 people—there would be more later—this was no ordinary meal, but Mama was undaunted by the numbers. Preparations began well in advance. Spicy pumpkin pies, mouth-watering lemon with inch-high meringue the color of baked biscuits, one after another they came hot from the oven of the old wood range.

Delightful odors of chocolate fudge and penuche candy filled the kitchen. There had to be bowls of ruby red cranberry sauce, which Papa wouldn't touch, to add tang to the turkey which was the main attraction. We had it only twice a year, sometimes one large bird, sometimes two smaller ones. Once Pa made the mistake of buying such a huge one from Bill Meese that Mama had to chop the legs off it before she could fit it into the big roaster.

The dining table, ordinarily about eight feet long, was stretched out much farther with extension boards added, and a long kitchen table was added at the end. Sometimes the youngest children sat at a third small table. The sliding double doors leading to the adjoining bedroom could be opened to provide additional space.

What excitement for us children as we waited for each family group to arrive, often bringing additional pies, cakes or candy! Frank would come with his second wife Mary and children Ronald, Dolores and baby Gertrude, Mary came with her husband Joe Cabral and children Alfred and Madelyn, Joe with Adeline and children Nadine and Howard, Louise with her husband George Lawrence (Mama's youngest brother, no blood relation to Louise). Annie and her husband Manuel Lemos with their sons Clarence and Elwin were usually last to arrive—to us kids it seemed forever—for they lived in Ripon, at some distance in the Central Valley. Papa enjoyed seeing all his brood under one roof. Mama, too, was very glad to see them all and to know that through her efforts everyone was having such a good time. She never seemed to feel overworked or imposed upon.

We liked to hear all the news from everybody. Those were happy times and I'm sure none of us ever forgot them. After the meal all the women and girls pitched in, clearing the table, washing the dishes, and setting the house in order. Usually there were plenty of leftovers for people to take home to enjoy later.

Such pleasures were rare for it was farm work that shaped our lives. There was men's work and there was women's work. They were separate and well-defined. For Papa and his sons the yearly rhythm of the seasons—planting to harvest, birth to maturity, determined much of what they did and when they did it. For Mama and her daughters, cycles of work were repeated daily or weekly, over and over again.

Men's Work

FOR MEN ON the ranch there were two main lines of work, the raising of grain and animals, though plenty of other jobs had to be done. In both of these divisions the work varied according to the season of the year. Spring was the time of sprouting wheat and baby animals. Summer was the period of growth. Fall was harvest and breeding time. Winter was for hog-butchering and all those tasks that had been neglected in busier seasons, mainly repairs and construction.

Men using equipment drawn by teams of powerful draft horses did all the work on our farm at least until 1918 when Pa bought a tractor for Tiny, then about 20, to drive—Pa himself never felt comfortable with anything but horses. In early spring before the sowing of the wheat crop could begin, the ground had to be tilled. Papa had a cultivator with four rows of shares like small shovels that sped up the work. He also had an ordinary plow with one share that was more maneuverable for work around trees. Every year he plowed the orchard with the lines from the horse tied in a loop around his shoulders so his hands were free to guide the plow by the handles. A chicken or two followed behind, happily snapping up the worms that the plow dug up. I loved to watch the plowshare turning over long, gleaming slabs of our black earth, which shone like polished steel.

In fact, I never tired of watching my father work the soil, whether he was using a plow or cultivator to turn it, a harrow or clod masher to break it up, or a roller to smooth it. The harrow, a large-toothed version of a rake, broke up the clods. The cultivation not only got rid of weeds but oxygenated the soil and helped the winter rains seep down to the roots of the trees. We did not irrigate and California summers are dry. Once in a while after the ground was cultivated, a roller called a clod masher was run over the ground to flatten the clods still further. About half of our 640 acres was prepared for planting.

Then Papa would hitch up a team to the seed sower. It had a funnel-shaped hopper on top from which seed dropped down onto a revolving, vaned disc, a sort of fly wheel, which could cast wheat or barley over the plowed ground faster and more efficiently than a human arm. If the sowing was done in the dim early morning, poor Ev would have to "track" before she went to school, riding Captain along the edge of the last path sowed so that Pa could see where to sow the next one.

The sown fields soon sprouted. A faint green mist spread over the brown hills, then turned a rich emerald green. The wheat grew tall and thick in the hot summer sun. In October, when the heavy heads of grain turned golden, the harvest would begin. Papa had made ready in advance by sharpening the mower blades on his foot-pedal-operated grindstone, for the blades had to be sharp to cut down the grain. I remember helping him by holding up one end of a mower blade while he sharpened the other. Water was dripped onto the stone in the process to keep the blade from overheating.

The mower had a long, composite cutting blade made up of a series of sharp-edged triangles that traveled in a swath back and forth to cut the stalks. The newly cut hay was raked up into long windrows by a rake shaped like a twelve-foot long comb with curled, arm-length metal teeth that looked like an extra-wide hand with a row of spread fingers all the same length. After a few days, workmen would run a buck-rake from one end of the windrow to the other, gathering the hay into shocks.

A man tidied up the shocks with a pitchfork and then a big hay wagon was driven into the field. One of its sides was about five feet high, the other about two feet lower so men could more easily pitch hay onto it. Most of the hay, load after load, was taken away to form a huge stack in a convenient location for threshing or hay baling. Some of the loose hay would be stored in the barns as feed for the cows and horses.

When I was about sixteen, Tiny and Bert having left the ranch to go out on their own, it was I who had to drive old Kate, the fork-horse who lifted loose hay into the barn. A big fork was loaded up with hay from the wagon. It was tied to a long rope which ran through a pulley attached to the roof of the barn and then down to a singletree, a wooden bar attached to Kate's harness. When she walked away from the barn, she lifted heavy loads up through an opening into the hayloft. I walked along beside her. But then when the fork was empty she had to back up to the place she had started from, and she didn't like that. She would just stand there and refuse to move. I had to pull on the reins and haul her back by main force, again and again and again. I was only five feet two and about 118 pounds, but I was strong. Still, that was the heaviest work I

The hay wagon, 1922. Bert left, Joe Peters right.

ever had to do on the ranch.

Sometimes Papa used a binder instead, which was like a mower with special equipment attached for binding the bundles of hay. I'm not exactly sure how it worked but it had a sort of platform for catching the loose hay and it produced sheaves of hay tied into bundles with binding twine. All kinds of equipment were needed on the farm (my father's was usually the

Joe Peters cutting hay with a binder, 1922.

John Deere brand) so his farming operation required a considerable capital investment. He had little bargaining power in the sale of cash crops, hogs and especially cattle. He usually had to take whatever a stock buyer offered because waiting for a better price was too costly. Every extra day he had to feed his cattle cut into his profits. Still, he prospered.

When the harvest was in, a hired threshing machine and crew arrived at the farm at a designated time to do the work. The threshing was a thrilling sight. A steam engine with a long, wide revolving belt powered the machine. When bundles of hay were fed into the thresher, a heavy stream of grain would come pouring out of its side into the gaping mouth of a gunny sack. A man stood guard there and sewed up the filled sacks with a large needle and twine. They were then stacked into a huge pile. My parents must have been thrilled to see that mountain of wheat! It was the culmination of a year's work.

Threshing machine and hired crew, Bollinger Canyon, about 1901.

The arrival of the haypress and its crew was another exciting event, more amusing to a child than any of today's movies.
A cook wagon equipped with a wood stove came along with
the haypress and was parked in the Big Yard. My cousin Isabel
Victorino, a daughter of Mama's sister Annie, was the cook, so
Ev and I got invited into the tiny kitchen to see the huge roasts,
pots of beans, homemade loaves and other hearty food that she
prepared there for those she called her "mens."

The men who fed the press had to be in top physical condition, like football players, to do such hard labor. They
worked stripped to the waist and sweating profusely, feeding
big charges of hay into the maw of the machine, which
clamped them all down in a bale-sized mold. Another charge

Threshing crew and grain harvest, Bollinger Canyon, about 1901. Joe Peters top, fourth from left; Joe, Jr. first row, second from right.

was added and compressed as before, and another and another until a complete bale was formed. Wires were then poked through the slats in the cage and wrapped around the bale in several places. These were big, heavy bales about 4½ by 3½ by 2 feet. To move one, a worker would grasp in each hand a wooden-handled hook made especially for the purpose. He would jam one hook into each end of the bale and heave away.

All the bales were piled into a very large and impressive looking stack that told of a bountiful harvest. Later they would be loaded onto a flat-bed wagon and hauled either to the hay storage barn that had been added next to the horse barn, or to a warehouse in San Ramon where they would be kept until sold.

In winter, when grass in the pasture grew scarce, the cattle needed some hay as supplementary feed, so Papa would hitch up a horse to a flat sled and go to the hay barn to get it. Using bale hooks he would heave a couple of bales, one on top of the other, onto the sled and then take them out to the fields. Once there, he'd hack at the wire bindings with a dull axe and the bales would burst open. Then he'd break them up into charges and spread them around with a pitchfork so that hay was accessible to all. Papa's cattle, in fact all of his animals, were always well fed.

They were well watered, too. California's long dry season made wells and the windmills that brought up the water essential and Papa was careful to keep them in good repair. Luckily, both were already installed on the Butcher and Palmer ranches when Papa bought them. By that time the drilled well in a steel casing was as much as 300 feet deep. Without wells, cattle ranching would have been impossible on that dry soil. I remember hearing a friend of Papa's trying to convince him that water could be located by a method in which you walked back and forth over the land extending in front of you a forked stick held loosely in both hands. If it began to wiggle the water was found and you dug there. This was called water-witching. Pa just listened politely and then ignored the whole idea. He had too much common sense to believe in such a tale.

The part of the animal growth cycle that had to do with procreation and birth in anything bigger than a chicken must have been carefully concealed from us girls for I have no memories at all of such things. The baby animals signaled each new year for us, and how we enjoyed them! As they grew we lost some of our interest in them, although the twice-yearly cattle roundup, with the animals jostling in the corral, was exciting.

Tiny bucking hay bales, 1922.

In later years the roundup often became the occasion for a family reunion and picnic. At the roundup young males were castrated so they would develop into steers (beef animals), not bulls, although of course we never witnessed that procedure either.

Then they all had to be branded. In the early days Papa simply cut off the tip of one of their ears and made a two-inch slit in the other, probably believing that the ears weren't overly sensitive to pain. Later he had a blacksmith make him a branding iron with a monogram of his initials, JP. Still, I never once heard of anyone losing any cattle to theft.

A more ominous threat to the cattle was a disease called blackleg. I remember how alarmed my parents were when they heard that local ranchers were beginning to lose animals. Every year from then on, everyone, including Papa, had to vaccinate against it although, luckily, we never lost any of our steers to the disease.

The cattle did sometimes meet with accidents, however, so Papa was always checking on them. Frank used to say that Pa had such keen eyesight that he could count them as they grazed on the faraway Butcher Ranch hills, though usually he went out on horseback to look after them. Once a young heifer somehow jumped into a manger and couldn't get out. Though Pa managed to free her, the poor thing had suffered irreparable damage. Her head was twisted at a freakish angle so she couldn't graze. Since her flesh was in no way harmed, he sold her to the local butcher.

Another accident happened to a steer who fell into our drinking water reservoir. When the water from the faucet looked muddy, Papa sent Ev up there to see why. She ran home all excited to say that a steer had broken through the fence and the boards covering the reservoir and had fallen in. I don't know how Pa and Tiny rescued it. Perhaps they tied a noose around its horns and made a work horse pull it out.

Milk cows were a source of regular income, whereas beef cattle took a long time to get ready for market. Mama told me that the family, with the help of a hired man, milked a string of ten or twelve cows for ten years and did very well at it. By the time I went to high school in 1919, they kept only a couple of cows for family use. In the cow corral, next to the milk house, a huge metal tank stood on a wooden platform. A long step along one side made it easy for the milkers to climb up to empty their pails into the tank. A spigot at the bottom of the tank ran the milk into twenty-gallon cans that were taken into the milk house, where the cream was separated.

A steam engine powered the separator. It was Tiny's job to feed firewood into the engine to keep the pressure up, and watch the gauge. I had a healthy respect for that demonic engine. Papa always warned Tiny never to let the pressure go too high. Didn't he say over and over that he used to know someone named Joe Lewis who had blown himself up? Tiny must also have been impressed by this story for, reckless as he was, both he and the engine came through unscathed.

As the milk entered the separator, it came in contact with a series of spinning discs or "pans" housed in a cylinder. The cream, lighter in weight, rose to the top of the cylinder where it was expelled through a spout. Skim milk, being heavier, was ejected through a lower spout. Cream went into a twenty-gallon can, skim milk into another. Periodically, a man came to take away the cream for butter, having tested it first for its fat content. Skim milk was never wasted but was fed to the hogs. It is hard to believe that nowadays, cholesterol-conscious consumers pay just about as much for skim as for whole milk. I think my parents stopped milking all those cows about the time Cousin John Soares left the ranch to go off on his own. He was so skilled, he could not easily be replaced.

Our horses were central to farm life as they did most of

the work. They needed regular currying and grooming. Papa always took them to the blacksmith in Danville to be shod, because it was work he didn't like to do. Although we had our own blacksmith shop with a forge and anvil, our men did only metal work and tool sharpening there.

Straw for bedding the horses was tossed down from an opening in the platform ceiling above their stalls. The used bedding straw together with accumulated manure had to be removed each day, so Papa or one of his sons or the hired man would take a pitchfork and toss it through the small front windows. A slight steam arose from the growing heap along with the characteristic manure odor as heat from the oxidation developed. Our hens seemed to enjoy scratching there, and the rooster would stand on top like king of the mountain. When you approached the barn you never failed to smell the manure pile, not really an unpleasant odor. It was a perfect organic fertilizer, much better than the ersatz stuff used nowadays. Wagonloads of manure would be driven into the fields and scattered with a pitchfork, for a good farmer husbands the soil. Papa used no sprays either. He didn't know then that ours was an organic farm. It was the only kind of farming he knew.

Pa kept a sharp eye out for noxious weeds, especially thistles, and cut them out before they could set seed and spread. If neglected they would take over a large area. A few horseradish plants were in the orchard when he bought the home place but the patch gradually increased in size as the yearly plowing broke up the roots and spread them around. Since we never ate horseradish they were a nuisance. But one day some entrepreneur drove by, saw the plants and offered to buy them. Pa happily agreed.

Papa always killed three hogs at intervals during the winter. He learned how to do it at home in Beira, where the yearly slaughter of the family hog was an important and necessary tradition. Since we had no refrigeration it had to be a cold day so the meat wouldn't spoil. He'd stab the pig in the throat, severing an artery, and at least once he caught the blood for blood sausage. Next he had to dip the carcass into the big black witches' cauldron, the water not quite boiling so as to avoid cooking the meat—first one end and then the other, in and out. He then made a slit behind each hind leg tendon so he could insert a special gadget between the legs that let him string up the hog with block and tackle. With a heavy butcher knife, not too sharp, he carefully scraped off all the bristles, then washed the carcass. Next he slit the animal down the belly, removing the heart and liver and letting the guts fall out into a washtub. I remember our making the traditional linguiça sausage only once. That time sister Mary bravely volunteered to wash out the guts.

The hog was hung from a tree limb overnight so it would chill. The next morning Papa would carry it to the big heavy table in the meat room off the bunkhouse so he could cut it up. He set aside as much fresh meat as could be used for the table—roasts, chops, spare ribs and the like—and prepared the hams and bacon for salting and then smoking. The fat, including the leaf lard that surrounded the guts, he cut into cubes for rendering out in the oven. The resulting lard would be stored in big crocks in the basement where it would chill and keep fresh all winter long.

Tiny, Bert and Ed were full participants in all the work. Papa took it for granted that any children still at home would work for the family but our brothers had it a lot harder than we girls did. They had to work like men from an early age. Not surprisingly, all of them could hardly wait until they were old enough to escape from the long hours of labor on the farm and go off on their own.

My father was balding, gray-bearded, short and strong. The fingers on his big hands were thickened and gnarled from years of heavy labor. When I picture him in my mind's eye I see him in an old felt hat, a woolen coat jacket of dark, grayish material and heavy cotton work pants of a nondescript dark gray, possibly once black but faded by time and countless scrubbings on a washboard with strong, brown Mikado brand soap. He worked outdoors in all weathers and he wore what he was comfortable in. To keep warm in the winter cold, he had two-piece underwear—shirts and long-johns of a heavy, rib-knit woolen material. I always thought his coat was what was left of a suit that was no longer good enough for church or funerals but still had some wear left in it. That would have been in keeping with Papa's frugal ways yet he seldom if ever wore out a suit. Probably, Mama ordered his work clothes from the Sears and Roebuck catalog or bought them from Massa's dry goods store in Hayward.

When I picture Pa he is always busy—with the animals or the farm machinery or working with his sons at all the jobs that must be done around a farm, especially in the slack season after harvest: fence building, road graveling, tree grafting and pruning, mending harness, treating the wheat with bluestone to prevent smut, cutting and stacking wood for the stove, building a shed or digging a septic tank. Woman had her work and man had his. I never saw my father do a lick of work

Ed Peters, 1922, age 19.

around the house except things like changing the washer in a faucet now and then, or cleaning out the gutters, or lowering a load of bricks tied in a gunny sack down the chimney to clean out the soot. But mess around in the kitchen? Never. Pa had plenty of his own work to do and Ma had hers.

Women's Work

THE WHOLE FAMILY went to bed soon after the dinner dishes were done, as the new day would begin at four or five the next morning, depending on the season. We had to get up earlier when putting in or harvesting crops. Pa would light the coal oil lantern and set off to feed the horses; they had to have their breakfast while we had ours. Ma would put newspapers and kindling in the old wood stove, then add sticks of firewood from the big wood box next to the stove. The world outside might be white with frost but until the fire got going there would be no heat in that cold house.

Ma's mind ticked off the chores as she did them: Grab the heavy butcher knife and slice the home-smoked bacon, cut off the rinds and lay the strips in a pan with cold water just to cover; heat it up but not to boiling so as to remove excess salt; now drain and fry. Fill up the huge agate ware coffee pot with a gallon of water, add hand-ground coffee and set it on the stove until it's just about to boil. Add a dash of cold water to settle the grounds. Boil up some water in a great pot, add salt and throw in a bunch of oatmeal from the Hornby's Oatmeal package. Reheat the fried red beans. Pa won't eat them but Bert has to have them at every single meal. Keep turning the bacon until nicely brown and crisp, drain and put it on a platter in the warming oven. Now, in the bacon grease, fry a lot of eggs fresh from our own hens, basting them as they fry. Slice the homemade bread and put it on the kitchen table; it needs no toasting and anyway we have no toaster. Put out our fresh, home churned butter, homemade quince jelly and a pitcher of milk from our own cows for the oatmeal.

For yesterday's breakfast we might have had stacks of pancakes instead of bread, with rich, brown, maple-flavored syrup poured on from a monstrous tank of a syrup can. Tomorrow we may substitute a big pan full of milk toast (*sopas de laite* or milk soup in Portuguese), made from stale bread covered with hot milk and sprinkled with sugar and plenty of cinnamon. Some days it might be French toast with butter and sugar or jam.

After breakfast, Pa would go outside and Ma would get right to work. First and foremost on her list of jobs was the task of providing meals for the family and the farm workers. Food for hardworking men had to be substantial, nourishing, and as tasty as possible. And it had to be ready on time, whether served at home, as was usually the case, or at the Butcher Ranch, or out in the fields at harvest time. Ma was expert at this.

Three big meals were served daily—breakfast, the midday dinner and supper at night. In addition, when they were doing exceptionally heavy labor like harvesting, a high-calorie second lunch would be taken to the field in mid-afternoon for the men in our family and the hired crew. The men would be sitting or lying around on the ground as in a Brueghel painting when Ma arrived in her sunbonnet with a basket over her arm. In it she carried slabs of her own bread and huge hunks of

A second lunch in the field, 1922. Rose at right.

cheddar cheese. I would come behind her with homemade doughnuts and a pot of hot coffee. How good that must have tasted after all that hot, hard work!

It took great quantities of food to feed the eight or nine people who usually sat at our table. Many of the staples, such as hams, bacon, eggs, milk, butter, potatoes, and certain other vegetables came from the farm itself, along with an occasional chicken. Whenever possible, supplementary food was bought in large quantities, which not only saved money but the time and energy of trips to town with a horse-drawn wagon. Considerable storage space was necessary. 100 pound sacks of flour and sugar were stored in large tip-out bins in the pantry, where they were handy for Mama's bread-and-biscuit-making. A fifty pound barrel of coffee beans was stored in the cellar, adjacent to the hand-turned coffee grinder and the churn, for we performed both jobs in the cellar. Hundred pound sacks of pink beans were also kept there, as were dried prunes, potatoes, cheese, and crocks of our own lard. A screened meat safe where we stored our fresh meat dangled from the ceiling; we had no ice-box in those days.

Summers were time for home canning, and hot work it was. Mama canned tomatoes as well as the peaches, plums and pears from our own orchard, and she made quince jelly. At first these fruits were literally canned, for she put them up in old-style tin cans, first filling the can with hot, cooked fruit, then fitting a shallow lid with a projecting rim over a projecting rim on the can, after which heated rosin was poured around the edges to seal in the contents. Later she used mason jars with zinc screw tops and a rubber gasket, a great improvement.

As in most old-time houses, much of the kitchen work went on in a small, attached pantry which contained the sink and its rippled wooden drainboard, storage cabinets for food and pots and pans with work counters above, large bins for flour and sugar, and shelves for everyday dishes. Mama's kitchen certainly wasn't as organized and convenient as are many modern ones. The stove, with its attached tank for heating hot water, was at least eight feet away from the pantry on the far side of the large kitchen. The kitchen table was across from the stove. In the corner of the kitchen was the door that led down concrete steps to the cellar. Every move among these basic work elements took many steps.

Although we were largely self-sufficient, we counted on people who came to the door to sell us things we couldn't or didn't want to produce for ourselves. The butcher wagon came around twice a week. Rather like a large box, it had doors in back and carried ice inside to keep the meat cold. The owner,

Mr. Joe Lawrence (no relation to my mother), the local butcher, no doubt sold us back some of the beef that Papa had sold to him. Though our family butchered pigs, killing a steer was too big a project for us. Ev and I liked to accompany Mama to the butcher wagon because usually we would walk away from it nibbling on a slice of bologna the butcher had given us. Old-fashioned bologna was made with lardoons, or strips of fat, running through it. I always picked out the bits of fat and threw them away. Ma usually bought a large roast and a steak which she would pan-broil for supper that evening in the large iron frying pan. I don't know which was more delicious—the steak itself or the gravy that was made from the pan drippings. I'd break up a slice of bread on my plate and smother it with that wonderful gravy. The roast would be served the next day at the big noon dinner. In fact, It was enough for two or three meals. What was left over was usually reheated in the oven or served with a sauce made of fried onions mixed with water and a little vinegar, a Portuguese taste.

I well remember how Mama made hash, which I loved. The recipe called for equal quantities of raw potatoes and left-over roast pork, along with a lesser amount of onions, all of which were coarsely chopped—she used a large wooden bowl and a special, crescent-shaped, two-handled chopper made just for this purpose. Finally, all the ingredients were mixed with left-over gravy and baked in the oven. Simple but delicious!

The fish man came on Friday, the fast day for local Catholics. I remember that the flounders were delicious, though it seemed freakish that both their eyes were on one side, the top side. Other types were less tasty—barracuda, for example. As the fish man didn't carry the salt cod *(baccalá)* that is a Portuguese favorite, we bought that at the general store. It was sold in petrified sheets that had to be soaked in lots of water before being boiled, flaked and made into a sort of hash with onions and potatoes.

It may seem strange, but we bought many of our vegetables from a vendor who delivered them to the door. The farm operation took so much time that Pa couldn't give a lot of attention to his garden. The vegetable man was a middle-aged Italian with black sparkling eyes and magnificent mustachios that curled up on the ends. Papa used to refer to him as *"O gaitado"* (the bagpipe player), because he was given to sudden, startling bursts of shrill laughter at the slightest provocation. The variety of vegetables he carried was limited but he always had cabbage, carrots, turnips, beets, iceberg lettuce, string beans and sometimes peas—no exotics like artichokes, asparagus, or even broccoli.

Mama cooked on a big, black wood stove. It really was black as we bought stove polish to give a gunmetal sheen to everything but the shiny nickel scrollwork trim that supported the warming oven over the stove top. I detested that trim. One of my jobs was to clean it and, because of all the frying we did, it always collected a lot of grease which had to be laboriously picked out of the crevices. While they may look less picturesque, I appreciate the smooth, easy-to-clean surfaces of today's stoves.

Mama baked bread at least twice a week but if we seemed to be running out she could turn out a pan of hot biscuits or cornbread in no time at all. To make her bread, she would take a dry cake of Fleischman's yeast and soak it in the water in which some potatoes had cooked. She'd set the mixture on top

Sears, Roebuck nickeled steel cooking range, 1907. A porcelain-lined reservoir (water heater) is attached at right.

of the stove's warming oven for a time, to "develop," before mixing it with flour and salt in a dishpan. The finished dough was covered with a dishcloth and a blanket and left to rise in a warm place by the stove. Then she punched it down, shaped it into five loaves, and let it rise once more. Finally, she placed all five in a big, black pan about twenty inches square, three loaves vertically along one side, two horizontally along the other. It was good bread, too, substantial bread, and fit for the gods when hot from the oven. I thought nothing in the world smelled as good as Mama's bread baking.

All the while we children were growing up, Mama washed clothes for eight or nine people, sometimes including a hired man. We had no built-in laundry tubs, though water was piped into the washroom in the bunkhouse. Every Monday big round galvanized tubs were placed on a bench and filled with hot water from the faucet. She rubbed the wet clothes with strong brown Mikado bar soap, then scrubbed them clean on a washboard. Dirty water was emptied into a sump—a wooden box sunk in the ground in a corner of the washroom, from where the water was piped out into the orchard.

I shudder now when I think of all the filthy overalls, sweaty shirts, heavy winter underwear, dresses, sheets and towels that Mama scrubbed by hand. When I got old enough I used to help her but I was never as good at it as she was. Modern women have no idea what housework used to be. I do barely remember that she once bought some sort of a washing machine before we had electricity. Inside a wooden tub was a kind of dolly with wooden fingers on it that served as an agitator. But it was soon discarded, either because it didn't get the clothes clean or because it had to be laboriously operated with a crank.

We had no bleach. To get them white, sheets, pillowcases, dishtowels and such were placed in soapy water in a copper wash boiler and brought to a boil on the wood range in the kitchen, then were stirred and lifted with a three-foot length of broomstick.. Small, marble-like balls of bluing were tied in a cloth and swished around in the last of the rinse waters. The clothes were wrung out by hand.

We all wore cotton almost exclusively, with just an occasional woolen. We never dry-cleaned anything, if indeed dry cleaning existed then; certainly I never heard of it. Our gingham dresses had to be starched. Lumps of cornstarch were dissolved in cold water, then the mixture was stirred into boiling water to cook and thicken it. The clothes were dipped in the resulting gruel-like paste. The next day, Mama ironed our school dresses flat on the blanketed kitchen table. When we put them on, the sleeves were always glued together with starch so that we had to push our arms through.

Tub loads of clothes were carried from the washroom, and clamped with one-piece clothespins on the backyard clothes-lines to dry. We girls were often called on for this job. I remember that women's underpants had to be doubled before hanging so they couldn't be recognized for what they were. Ev and I called them "Mama's bologna pants" because of a fancied resemblance to the sausages. The knee-length legs of this gar-ment were not sewn together; rather, both were attached to a waistband and the crotch was left open all the way from front to back. This was convenient given the absence of elastic but it may seem strange for women who were so excessively modest that their underpants couldn't be openly hung on the line.

Tuesday was ironing day. Ma did her ironing on a work table kept opposite the stove. When she wanted to iron she would pull the table up closer to the stove, where her weighty sad irons were heating up. There were two types of sad iron (the dictionary says the adjective means "compact, heavy" in this context). One was pointed at both ends and had a detachable wooden handle. The other was wedge shaped with an attached iron handle. She had to keep the wood fire going all the time she was ironing, even on hot summer days, though I never heard her complain about it. Still, she was happy later when she got an iron that was heated by some sort of fuel. She attached a bicycle pump to the iron and pumped it to produce gas, which had to be ignited to give off heat.

Mama always sewed most of our clothing on the old boxed-in pedal sewing machine she got from Sears and Roebuck —dresses, slips, nightgowns, even muslin underpants. Our long black stockings and the short Ferris waists (a sort of vest) to which garters were attached came from Sears as did our winter coats and ready-made men's clothes and socks. We went to Hayward for shoes.

I learned to mend socks by watching how Mama did it, and then it became my job. First she pulled the sock over an egg-shaped wooden darner with a handle on it, which made the task much easier. Then she did a sort of weaving job to fill in the hole. Nowadays, of course, time is money and socks are cheap. Most people don't hesitate to toss a holey one away. Ma would have been appalled by such waste.

One of my very earliest recollections is of Mama carding wool from our few sheep so it could be used in making comforters. The two cards were like flat, rectangular, wire-bristled brushes with handles. Ma placed a handful of prewashed wool on one of them, then rubbed the two together so as to flatten and smooth the fibers, making them run parallel. For the quilt making itself, a wooden quilting frame was set up at one end of our big dining-room. A large rectangle of cloth was attached to it, a layer of wool or cotton was spread on top, and a second cloth rectangle was placed above that and basted in place. Then Mama or I began at one end to do the quilting. An arc or shell-like pattern of stitching was easiest to do. After we had finished a few rows there was a way of rolling up that end of the quilt for easier access to the rest.

Raising chickens and turkeys was always Mama's responsibility. Of course we girls helped by feeding and watering them and gathering the eggs, and one of us kids always cleaned the hen house. I remember once Ma brought home a rooster, I think from one of her sisters. I guess she wanted to improve the stock. Now and then lice would get on the chickens and then she would dab a little mercuric ointment on the bald spot under each wing. I don't know who taught her to do that.

Chickens were an occasional treat that Mama would serve for dinner either fried or roasted with bread and giblet stuffing. It bothered us a little to see Mama kill one. She would tie its feet together, then suspend it from a fence post. Next she would grasp its head in her left hand, take a sharp, heavy knife in her right and slit its throat. Farm women had to learn things that few modern women would even think of doing.

Then the hen would have to be plucked. She would have ready a pot of boiling water, which she would temper by adding a bit of cold to it so as to avoid cooking the flesh. A bath in hot water made the feathers, even the pin feathers, easy to remove. (Often she would wash and dry the choicest of the feathers and use them for making pillows.) Next she would cut the chicken open near the vent and pull out the entrails, saving the liver, gizzard and heart. She carefully cut away from the liver a small green sac, the gall bladder, whose contents must never touch the liver lest it taste "as bitter as gall."

She was also in charge of the baby calves, who had to be weaned from their mothers as soon as green grass was added to their diet. It was Mama's job to teach them one by one to drink from a bucket. She would back the calf into a specially made stall in a corner of the calf shed and clasp her hand over its nose, keeping her fingers in its mouth. When the calf began sucking on them, she would lower its head into a bucket of milk so it got a taste. Then, gradually, she would pull her fingers away. Soon it would be drinking milk all by itself.

When a pig had been killed and Papa had hung the hams and bacon in the smokehouse, it was Mama's job to build a fire under them and keep it burning. She would start the fire with dry wood, then place a green log on top. When the log began burning it would produce smoke. Then Ma inverted over it an old washtub with a hole in it. The log would smolder all day.

For a few years we were not selling cream and were only milking one or two cows to provide milk and butter for the family. We didn't use a separator then. During this period, Mama used to set out on the counter several large pans of milk to allow the cream to rise to the top. She would remove the cream with a skimmer which resembled a tin saucer with a handle and holes in the bottom, as her mother had done at the Wood ranch, years before. To make our butter we used a small hand operated wooden churn with beaters inside. When we girls became old enough we did this ourselves. I remember that it was tiresome work to turn that thing, small as it was, so that I looked with awe at the gigantic churn that lay abandoned in the yard, left over from the old milking operation in Bollinger Canyon.

As World War I approached and finally came in 1917,

cream was selling at a high price so Mama restarted the milking operation. It came at a good time for she was trying to earn money to send Ed to the University of California. When I went to high school, I helped her save for Ed's board and room and tuition fees. In the morning before school, I would milk at least one cow and then help Mama turn the crank of the hand-operated separator she had bought. It took two of us to do it, she pumping on one side of the long handle and I on the other. Afterward there was the job of cleaning up the milk pails as well as the series of pans and other working parts of the separator. All had to be meticulously washed at the big wooden sink in the corner of the milk house, a tedious job that always fell to Mama as I had to hurry off to school. Periodically, a man with a truck came to haul away the cream to the dairy.

We girls had to carry a fair share of the housework. It was simply expected of us. and we never complained about what was just a tiny fraction of our mother's chores. Any work around the house was girls' work, though Ed did take turns with Ev and me in filling the wood box or churning butter. He also had the unpleasant job of emptying the sludge from the container that made the acetylene gas for the gas lights, in addition to helping Pa with whatever outdoor chores were suitable to his age, like feeding, watering and currying the horses, or cleaning out stables. Ev and I had to wash and dry the evening dishes, set the table, feed the chickens, gather the eggs, churn the butter, grind the coffee, bring in wood for the range and the heater, empty the ashes, empty and scald out the chamber pots, sweep the kitchen, hang out and take in the clothes, make our own school lunches, and fetch and carry. My own special jobs were polishing the stove, cleaning the coal oil lamps, and sewing and mending.

Once my sewing skills were applied to mending gunny sacks in advance of the wheat threshing season. Bundles of sacks were suspended by baling wire from the granary rafters. One such bundle evidently harbored a mouse who industriously gnawed a hole through the lot of them. I had to mend each one by sewing on a patch with a sack needle and twine. This was a lot of extra work, so it was the only job for which I was ever paid. I think I earned a penny a sack. As five cents would buy a whole bag of candy at Hurst's General Store in San Ramon I was temporarily rich. Mr. Hurst kept his jars of candies on the very top shelf, away from little hands I suppose. There were lemon drops, raspberry drops, licorice, striped stick candy, and tiny candy hearts with mottoes like Oh You Kid, Be Mine, True Love, etc. They came in a fancy bag with narrow red and green stripes that added glamour.

By the time I reached high school I also had to saddle up Captain and bring in the cows from the upper pasture. Ev, when she was old enough, was assigned to ride over to the Butcher ranch and turn the windmill on, then ride back again to turn it off when enough water had been pumped for the cattle. Frances did more than we did because she was older, and at home full time. No need to make busy work for us; there was no end of the chores to be done. But it wasn't bad, not bad at all—I myself rather liked feeling part of a going concern. Life's not dull when things are humming.

Papa always said Mama was *"poupada"* (thrifty), a valuable and admired quality in any farm woman, especially perhaps in a Portuguese family, for in the Azores, where the specter of hunger always lurked, family survival may have depended on it. I learned thrift from both my parents. Once I made the mistake of throwing a crust of bread into the fire and Mama scolded that it was *wrong* to do that—I must always save scraps for the pigs or chickens. I felt it was almost like a sin to her. Certainly I never knew her to waste a bit of food of any kind; for a while she even rinsed off the dishes into a pail before she washed them with soap so she could throw the slop water to the hogs. And I remember that Papa once saw me hacking away at a pencil, trying to sharpen it. He took the knife out of my hands and showed me how to carefully shave the wood away to get a fine point without wasting the pencil.

Mama was a very small woman, not quite five feet tall and weighing maybe 105 pounds. Her deep-set golden-brown eyes and well-defined cheek bones gave her small, square face character and a hint of gauntness. Her hair, once black, grayed early. When I was a child she wore it long and pulled into a knot on top of her head. It was combed up over what was called a "rat," a sausage shape stuffed with some sort of fiber that gave an effect of fullness. Later, she cut her hair off in a short, no-trouble bob. Mama's everyday wear was a bib apron tied over a long gingham housedress, with high-top black shoes. Always busy, she walked quickly but with a decided limp and even standing still, one hip was markedly higher than the other. Mama was focussed. She had definite ideas as to how things should be done and she bustled around, wasting no time as she went about doing them.

People always admired Pa as a skilled and successful farmer, and rightly so. No doubt he was. But it irked me that Mama seldom got credit for the invaluable support she gave him and all that she contributed to her family. It was a man's

Joe and Rose Peters, about 1933.

world then and women's work never counted. It was taken for granted.

After lunch, when the season wasn't too busy, Pa would sometimes stretch out for a half hour's nap on the couch in the dining room, but I never in my life saw my mother stop to rest unless she was too sick to work. There was always something that needed doing. One time in the 1930's, when we all thought Ma was going to die from a serious case of pneumonia, Pa said to the doctor, intending to give her his very highest praise, "She did a lot of work in her time." And that she did.

San Ramon School Days

STARTING IN 1911 when I was not quite six years old I went to the San Ramon Grammar School, just as my ten older brothers and sisters had done before me, and as Evelyn, the last of us, would do in two more years. Once Evelyn was old enough to go with me, we walked to school together, a little less than a mile. In good weather we enjoyed the walk. In our starched gingham school dresses, our long, black, ribbed cotton stockings and sturdy brown high-topped shoes, we marched along the graveled dirt road, swinging our lunch pails by their bails. Empty lard cans they were, with a logo of two green leaves printed over the name Leaf Lard (now and then when the lard from our own hogs ran out Mama would buy canned lard from the store).

We walked past our horse barn, across a wooden bridge over a small creek and up the hill. To our left, at some distance, tree-studded San Ramon Creek meandered through Anderson's pasture land. Behind the creek, hidden behind the trees, lay our Butcher Ranch and adjoining Palmer Ranch. On the right, from low gently rolling pasture land, our Home Ranch gradually ascended to the wooded crest of the Las Trampas range. Meadow larks sang in the fields, and redwing blackbirds swung on yellow-flowered mustard stalks. We went on, past the George Oswill family's flatlands and their house, past the deserted Protestant church, until we arrived at the schoolyard.

Sometimes we would get caught in the rain on our way to school. Then we would have to dry out our woolen caps, coats and shoes near the wood burning heater at school, for we had no raincoats, overshoes or umbrellas. In winter time the mud puddles on the graveled dirt road were covered with ice. The ground felt frozen and so did our feet when we arrived. We toasted our toes at the heat of the wood stove but warming them too fast only resulted in the burning sensation of chilblains.

On really bad days my father would hitch up old Lily and drive us there. A shield of black waterproof cloth, stretched out in front and attached to the sides of the buggy, gave protection from the sleeting rain. Papa looked through a small window and held the reins that passed through a slot. How good it felt to be all snug and secure on the inside while the rain pelted away on the roof!

The village of San Ramon was then very small. As I remember it, clustered together near the corner of the Danville-San Ramon Road (now San Ramon Valley Boulevard) and the old Crow Canyon Road to the north of Bollinger Creek were Hurst's store and post office, the Community Hall, the school, Olsson's blacksmith shop and the jail, or calaboose as it was always called, a word derived from the Spanish *calaboso*. The latter was always empty though in earlier days it may have housed an occasional drunk. Then, south of the bridge over the creek, there were a saloon and Thorup's

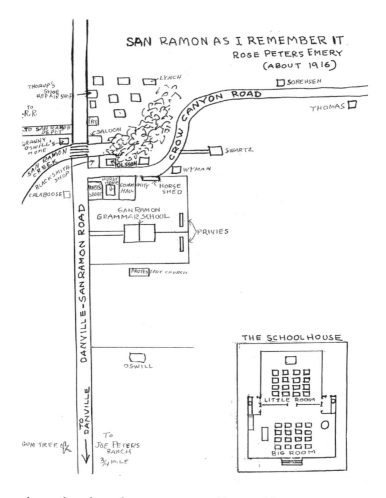

SAN RAMON AS I REMEMBER IT
ROSE PETERS EMERY
(ABOUT 1916)

THORUP'S SHOE REPAIR SHOP

LYNCH

SORENSEN

TO R.R.

THOMAS

TO SAN RAMON DEPOT

CROW CANYON ROAD

(RY)

SALOON

GRANNY OSWILL'S HOME

SAN RAMON CREEK

OLSSON

SWARTZ

BLACKSMITH SHOP

WYMAN

CALABOOSE

NURSE HOME

COMMUNITY HALL

HORSE SHED

MAROIS STORE

SAN RAMON GRAMMAR SCHOOL

PRIVIES

PROTESTANT CHURCH

DANVILLE-SAN RAMON ROAD

OSWILL

TO DANVILLE

THE SCHOOLHOUSE

LITTLE ROOM

BIG ROOM

GUM TREE

To JOE PETERS RANCH
3/4 MILE

shoemaker shop plus a scattering of houses. That was it.

The schoolhouse, a white wooden building with a small bell-tower on top and a flag pole above the entrance, sat in the center of a large field. Long benches where children could rest from play or sit to eat their lunches ran half the length of the schoolhouse on either side. A gravel path led up from the highway to the front steps, dividing the girls' yard on the right from the boys' yard on the left. Every morning, two by two and in perfect order, we marched up the steps and into the schoolroom to the beat of a drum played by one of the boys.

A high board fence extended from the back of the school-house to the rear fence, a further means of separating the boys from the girls. The privies were located along the back fence, one in the boys' yard, one in the girls'. As I remember, ours was a three-holer and below the seat was a long wooden trough with runners. A small wooden door on the side of the building permitted the trough to be dragged out on its runners so it could be hauled away to be dumped—horrors!—in the creek that ran through San Ramon. Later, more sanitary out-houses, chemical ones, were installed.

A wide wooden gate in the side fence opened into the boys' yard, and gave access to a long horse shed, open at the front. The teachers and any student who drove a cart to school or rode horseback, as did Dorothy Wilcox, would tie up to the shed's hitching rail.

It was a two-roomed school with one teacher in each class-room. Grades one through four were taught in the "Little Room" and grades five through eight in the "Big Room." Each teacher taught four grades but as there were only about 40 or 45 students in the entire school, all the classes were very small —I was one of only four in my eighth grade graduation class.

A bell like a church bell summoned us into the classroom. Located in the bell tower on the roof, its pull-rope dangled down near the door between the two rooms. The bigger boys eagerly vied for the job of ringing the bell in the morning and after recess. When we entered the schoolhouse we went first

San Ramon Grammar School

to the anterooms—the girls' on one side of the building, the boys' on the opposite side—where we stored our coats or jackets on hooks and our lunches on shelves. Every day of the year, Evelyn and I brought quince jelly sandwiches and a jar of home-canned fruit to school for our lunch. We made our own lunches and the jelly sandwiches were quick and easy to fix but we did get tired of them. I don't know why we never asked Mama for anything different. She certainly wasn't stingy with food and there was often leftover meat that would have made a tasty sandwich.

To drink, we had water from the school dipper. In each anteroom a small table held a bucket of drinking water and a communal dipper. Heaven only knows how many cases of mumps, measles and chicken pox were spread this way. Luckily we missed out on diphtheria and typhoid, though when I was two years old I came down with scarlet fever, possibly brought home by one of my older siblings.

The teacher's desk stood at the front of the room on a raised platform, this for better observation of the class, I suppose, and to symbolize authority. Behind the desk was a blackboard, a really black slate board, not the green composition chalkboards of today. Of course we had no fountain pens or ballpoints to work with, only steel pen points inserted into pen holders. A 1½ inch hole in the upper right hand corner of each desk held a small glass inkwell with rimmed top. The teacher poured ink into the wells from a large bottle with a spigot. Each of us was given a pink blotter with which to blot our finished papers. Parents often provided pen wipers made of several disks of heavy cloth of different sizes all stitched together in the middle. Mama showed me how to protect my books with homemade cloth covers. I still have the habit of covering books like dictionaries which I want to last.

My teacher in the Little Room, Blanche Wilson, a strict, no-nonsense kind of person, began by drilling us in phonics. Sounds in our primer were illustrated by pictures, like a snake with a darting tongue for the letter S. To show relations between words, Miss Wilson held up flash cards: C-AT, M-AT, R-AT, H-AT, etc. It was a very effective system, for we soon learned to sound out new words for ourselves and became good readers. We also read aloud every day. I doubt that Miss Wilson would have approved of the questionable look-and-guess system that some teachers later used and that left a student stranded when faced with new material. Phonics served me well later in life when I studied foreign languages. Sometimes we were lined up along a bench for a spell down. When you missed a word, you had to go to the end of the row and work up again. To prepare we were regularly given lists of spelling words to copy into our long, narrow copybooks. We had to know the meaning of every word. I always enjoyed these contests. Once I won a framed picture of Mt. Shasta as a spelling prize. I was really annoyed when I found out that my brother Tiny had removed the picture and replaced it with a likeness of one of his girlfriends. Probably he didn't even remember I had won it as a prize.

In the lower grades Miss Wilson would hold up an abacus in front of the class to teach addition and subtraction, or sometimes she called out a list of numbers we were to add in our heads, a procedure called "oral addition." Later, we learned arithmetic from a book entitled *Five Hundred Drill Problems,* which I don't remember being as bad as its name.

For making multiple copies of problems or other materials the teacher used a hectograph. This was a ¼ inch gelatin pad that covered the bottom of a shallow pan. A special kind of ink was used for the original copy. After the original was placed face down on the pad, it was carefully stroked with the fingers, which transferred the ink to the pad. A number of copies could then be made by pressing each sheet onto the master and smoothing it out with the fingers. When the ink wore off, the pad had to be cleaned and the whole tedious process repeated.

In the upper grades, grammar was emphasized, such things as parts of speech, declensions of nouns, and diagramming of sentences. This instruction, too, would help me later

San Ramon Grammar School, 1914. Teachers Ella Boucher, left, and Blanche Wilson. Evelyn seated, second from right; Rose standing far left; back row: Bert third and Ed sixth from left.

with learning and teaching foreign languages.

We were regularly assigned poetry to memorize: *Abou Ben Adhem, Thanatopsis, Hiawatha, The Charge of the Light Brigade, Annabelle Lee, The Village Blacksmith* and *O Captain, My Captain* are among those I still remember. But there was no school library, not even a handful of books, and I only remember a teacher reading a storybook to us once. *Ab, the Cave Man* was its name, and she read it a chapter at a time. For children with no radio, television, movies or storybooks it was as exciting as a Saturday matinee cliffhanger.

Discipline in school was rigidly enforced, and corporal punishment was expected. None of this "Stand in the corner" stuff in those days. I often heard reluctantly admiring tales from the older kids about the remarkable strength of one-armed Mr. Hodley, who would stuff a small troublemaker into a gunnysack and hang him on a peg in the wall. Another story held that before my time one of the teachers went so far as to keep a baseball bat in the anteroom in case of need. True or not, such stories were scarily fascinating.

One such story I do know to be true. Mr. Johnson, usually self-controlled, grabbed an older boy by the shoulders in exasperation and shook him so hard that the screws in the iron pedestal of the seat came loose from the wood floor, frightening the entire class into stupefaction. Fortunately such incidents rarely happened.

Miss Wilson was strict, too. On her desk was a tap-button bell at which she furiously banged away whenever anybody began whispering. It always startled the wits out of me so that it was hard to settle down to work again. And though I never saw her do it, she always threatened to tie a bit of cloth on a stick and swab out a liar's mouth with soap.

Sometimes, too, she used a ruler on the hands of erring students. Innocent students, too, I thought, the only time I was ever punished. She was asking the class, third-graders I think, to tell the meaning of proverbs. Question: "Rose, what is the meaning of 'A rolling stone gathers no moss'?" Answer, lamely given and with a nervous laugh because I'd never heard the expression before and suspected I didn't know what she was getting at: "Well, I suppose it means that the moss rubs off of a stone when it rolls down hill." Teacher's reaction: whack on the hand with the ruler. Did she think I was trying to be smart-alecky because I laughed? I wasn't, and though I know it's silly, I resent the punishment to this day. Anyway, that's when I first learned that words don't always mean literally what they say, something I had never encountered at home. It was my intro-duction to figurative speech.

Miss Wilson also kept on hand a small, tapering rawhide whip, a quirt, about four and a half feet long that she used on the pony that pulled her basket-cart. Years later my brother Ed told me that she once used this quirt on him and Ambrose Swartz for creating some sort of disturbance—or maybe just for whispering in class, since Ed was usually well-behaved. Afterward, hoping to prevent a repetition, they sneaked in and took the whip from a cabinet, carried it up into the hills and dropped it down a "dobie" crack (a deep split in the sun-dried adobe clay soil). They noticed a puzzled expression on Miss Wilson's face the next day when she discovered the loss, but she never said a word about it.

Because Tiny was older he was not in school with us but he, too, had had his troubles. Unlike Ed, he could be a real pain in the neck for a teacher, although from the kids' point of view he was lively and always good for a laugh. One of his favorite tricks was to place a noisemaking gadget between his knee and the underside of his desk. When the teacher's back was turned he would raise his knee sharply and make it squawk. Always, of course, with both hands innocently displayed on top of the desk.

I don't know what caused Tiny's worst debacle but he once came home from school with some really nasty stripes laid on across his back. Papa wouldn't have objected if he hadn't been punished so cruelly, but this was too much. No doubt Mama had her say about it too! Long afterward she told me that Papa went to the school in a fury and threatened to tear the man apart if it ever happened again.

Friday was my favorite day. Friday afternoons seemed more like play than work because then we had drawing, which I really enjoyed, and singing which I also enjoyed but wasn't as good at. Mrs. Boone, one of the mothers, came in to play the piano so everyone could sing songs like *My Country 'Tis of Thee, Yankee Doodle Dandy,* and Stephen Foster songs like *My Old Kentucky Home* and *Oh, Susanna.*

For Valentine's Day we were allowed to make valentines for our classmates, red hearts edged with paper lace. What fun! We also made paper chains for the school Christmas tree. One Christmas I made a jumping jack Santa Claus out of cardboard, which I was allowed to take home. This inspired me to go out and cut a limb off a madrone tree to make a small Christmas tree to hang it on—we had no evergreens with needles. This was the first and only Christmas tree in our house. Mama bought some candles and candle holders for it and stood by while we lighted them. She also bought a few ornaments, including two dazzling green birds with spun glass tails. I don't know what ever happened to them, those lovely birds that I so admired.

For a school play we once made a splendor of silver and gold stars, suspended by threads from the ceiling of the Community Hall where such functions were held. Whole big families came, with babies bedded down on the floor of the anteroom. I enjoyed these plays greatly, except for one time when I was disappointed to be selected as a winkie rather than a pinkie. The blonde girls, dressed in pink, were the good fairies; we brunettes, dressed in red, were the winkies or bad fairies.

Ed played the part of a monster called The Horned Homplice, with a headpiece made from a small nail keg with horns attached. I still remember the words he recited, to the delight of the audience:

> The Horned Homplice am I.
> I like to make little girls cry.
> I dig in my nails
> And laugh at their wails
> For the Horned Homplice am I.

In all, my experience at school was positive, and I am grateful to Miss Wilson for giving me a good foundation. Ed, too, told me not long before he died that he wished he had been able to go back to thank her. Evelyn, however, had a bit of difficulty when she entered first grade. Extremely shy, she just sat at her desk with her head down and wouldn't say a word in answer to the teacher's questions. Miss Wilson then asked me to tell her in Portuguese that she must answer. This I couldn't do for I couldn't speak enough Portuguese, so I whispered to her as low as I could so the teacher wouldn't hear me, "You have to do what the teacher says!" Ev knew she must obey —that's something we learned at home—so she did comply, and before long did very well in school.

Doubtless, Miss Wilson thought we spoke Portuguese at home because Papa still spoke English with a heavy accent and a limited vocabulary. But we didn't. My mother, having spoken only Portuguese at home, had experienced the difficulty of learning English at school. She tried to spare us that hardship by speaking English to us, so I could only say the names of things around the house and on the farm, although I understood a good deal more than that. Papa spoke to Mama in Portuguese sometimes, and I would hear him talking to the hired men or his nephew, John Soares, and I grasped a lot of what he said. I especially loved the old-country stories he would tell about witches *(feiticeiras),* ghosts, mysterious rappings and other eerie subjects.

It is possible that by speaking English my mother also wished to deny her heritage. Certainly she was keenly aware of the prejudice against Portuguese in some parts of the community. When she was in her nineties she told me that many years before, when she was riding through San Leandro on an "electric car," as streetcars were then called, one woman said to another in the seat ahead, "This looks like a nice town to live in." Mama was shocked by the insulting response, "Yes, but a lot of Portagees live here." She never forgot it.

In another play I was a Negro mammy dressed in an orange and red dress borrowed from Miss Wilson. My face was blackened with burnt cork and, unfortunately, when after the performance my mother washed my face in an available sink, the borrowed dress got slightly stained. Miss Wilson was hard put to conceal her annoyance. Of course she did not understand how anxious Mama was to get that black stuff off my face. At that time, before suntanning, great value was placed on fair white skin for women, which placed us olive-skinned Portuguese at a disadvantage. In order to keep our skins from being further darkened in the sun, Mama used to make sunbonnets for Ev and me but the sides were like blinders on a horse—you could only see straight ahead—so we sometimes accidentally let them fall off. Probably in the back of Mama's mind was the epithet "black Portagee," which was sometimes hurled at people in the heat of argument.

Prejudice of all kinds was, if not more widespread, at least more openly and unselfconsciously expressed in those days. One incident at school would never be tolerated now. A girl was allowed to recite a long comic poem in which every stanza ended with the boastful claim, "One dead-a da wop, 'cause I got the rock, I got the rock."

How we loved recess! The front fence was made with two rows of heavy pipe threaded through fence posts, and a long board placed over a pipe made a wonderful seesaw. But mostly the girls near my age played games that included everyone and required little or no equipment. Our group included Ev; Virginia Oswill and her sister Thelma with the golden curls; tall, slender Helen Read; Palmeda Ferreira, who miraculously sustained an aura of what might be called glamour; Petrea Thorup; friendly, sweet-faced Mary Mattos; and Dorothy Wilcox—she of the wondrous opal ring I so admired and the smelly bag of asafetida around her neck to ward off illness. We

San Ramon Grammar School, 1919, Rose's graduation year. Rose second from right, top row; Evelyn third from left, middle row; Ronald Peters, far left, bottom row.

played the old, traditional games of Drop the Handkerchief, Blind Man's Bluff, Farmer in the Dell, Ring Around the Rosy, hopscotch, marbles and jump rope, plus newer running/catching games called Cheese-it! and Dare Base. At noontime, when Mr. Johnson took your hand and ran you through the line of catchers in Dare Base, he went so fast your legs felt as if they were flying out behind!

After school, for a time, Father Galvin from St. Isidore's Catholic church in Danville used to park his flivver in the yard near the horse shed. When school let out, Ed and I would go and sit in the car with him and recite our catechism lessons in preparation for confirmation. Father Galvin was a kindly man and extremely devoted. Or at least I thought so, since he drove the five miles from Danville for just two kids.

Before we could be graduated, we had to pass final exams.

Even those of us who regularly got excellent grades couldn't help feeling anxious about them, and the teachers were anxious, too. During the exams a teacher would roam around and scan our arithmetic papers to see how we were doing. On one occasion, Mr. Johnson gave a loud harrumph and the student quickly scrambled to discover what he had done wrong. No doubt the reputation and maybe even the job of the teacher was dependent on the pupils' success.

Once in a while Superintendent of Schools Hanlon would visit the school. The teacher having warned us in advance to be on our best behavior, we sat like statues, hardly batting an eyelash during the whole ordeal. From this dignitary on graduation day in 1919, we four graduates received our big, gold-stamped diplomas, to which his honor's own august signature was affixed. Eighty-three years later, I still have mine.

Having Fun

MAMA MADE ONE of the few toys I ever had, a beloved cloth doll loosely stuffed with cotton, whose face was drawn with a pen. She herself never did own a doll. As a little girl she had to make do as best she could with a wine bottle dressed up in a gathered skirt. Not surprisingly, she was able to understand my longing for something more lifelike. I promptly christened the doll "Mushy" and loved her dearly for a long time. Unfortunately, poor Mushy came to a most inglorious end, for I dropped her down the hole of the outhouse and she was lost to me forever.

Not long after I had lost Mushy to the outhouse, a kindly man who worked for our neighbor John Baldwin, but who we girls had never met, came to the house with an unexpected surprise. Filled with the spirit of Christmas or, more likely, grateful for some favor from Pa, he brought presents for Evelyn and me. Since we seldom received any gifts, especially store-bought ones, this was an extraordinary event. Mine turned out to be a fancy little sewing basket lined with tufted pink sateen and fitted out with a thimble, needles, spools of colored thread, snaps, buttons, scissors and the like. It was pretty, yet I couldn't really appreciate it because Ev's gift was so much better—a beautiful doll with a porcelain head and real hair. Her waxen lids were fringed with eyelashes, something we had never seen before. Best of all, when you picked her up or laid her down, her eyes opened and closed.

The porcelain head was fitted on to a reasonably lifelike body of kidskin, but the difference in color and texture between the head and the cream-colored body bothered me. For this wasn't *total* make-believe like Mushy, but so nearly real that I felt it should look entirely real. I couldn't just let my imagination take over as Mama used to do when she dressed up a wine bottle. Still, that was just a tiny flaw, a mere nothing in such a beauteous creature. What worried us more was the knees. They didn't jut outward as knees should do. The manufacturer made the legs bend by slashing into each leg and putting in a gusset. They bent in the right direction but there was a wedge missing from the front of each knee and I couldn't avoid the uneasy feeling that our dolly was maimed. I say "our" dolly, for I played with her doll as much as Ev did, or at least as often as she would let me. When the knees made me too uncomfortable, I'd pull her dress down to cover them. My sewing basket was largely ignored in favor of the doll.

One of the reasons we had so few toys was that it wasn't the custom in our family to give presents on birthdays or at Christmas. Once, though, just before Christmas, Ev and I found two teddy bears in the trunk in Mama's bedroom, a small one meant for her and a larger one for me. We quickly closed up the trunk and never told Ma we had seen them, because we knew she meant them as a surprise. I remember, too, that we had a wooden top with a pull-string and used to play with it on the garden path.

We did most of our playing out of doors, but when the weather was bad we found things to do inside. We loved to rummage around in Mama's trunk. In it we found a tin name plate that had been removed from the coffin of her lost infant, little Louie, and his tiny funeral dress. The white dress was scattered with miniscule black sprigs. She kept outworn finery in there, like her remarkable mink and her wedding hat. It was big and drum-shaped, made from some soft, velvety material so dark brown as to be almost black. Two eleven-inch hat pins with tulip-shaped gold filigree ornaments pierced the fabric. We used those hat pins to beat out a staccato rhythm on the hat we named "*o tambor,*" the drum.

The alcove in our parents' room held a glass case, a sort of shrine, containing a small doll representing the Baby Jesus. It must have come from the Azores because, unlike American dolls, the baby was anatomically correct, as Ev and I were astonished to discover one day when we broke the rules and played with him. Perhaps for that reason, Frank's wife, Lizzie, had made him a ruffly little dress to wear.

Reading was not a possible amusement for us because, except for the Sears and Roebuck catalog, there were no books in our house. Nor any newspapers or magazines, for that matter. We didn't even own a Bible. The Catholic church didn't encourage Bible reading. Immigrant families like ours valued hard work and thrift, not pleasure or culture.

Once, however, when I was about eight, my brother Ed was operated on for appendicitis. His friend Roland Gass lent him some Oz books and Ed and I both read them avidly. Once I had picked one up I couldn't set it down. The Emerald City excited my imagination, and I remember well the beautiful and glamorous Ozma of Oz, who always wore a large flower on either side of her head. But one of the books had a story I could hardly bear to read. It was about a beautiful woman who changed her hairstyle each day by removing her head and putting on another. I looked with horror at the illustration of a row of heads, each one cut off at the neck and mounted on a short stick, waiting to be selected.

Ev and I often played outdoors in the garden. The white roses on the front fence were a thornless variety with dense foliage. They hung over the fence in a massive clump, forming a thick canopy with a dark, mysterious cave underneath, our secret place, where Ev and I could hide away from the world. Once Ed, Ev and I got into a sort of War of the Roses, snatching great handfuls of these fearful missiles and throwing them at each other. I think Ed was the eventual victor, and Ev and I retreated into our private cave to lick our wounds. Mama was probably too busy to notice the depredation to her garden, or if she did she didn't care for she never said anything. The roses would come back again next year.

One hot summer evening, the only time I can remember going barefoot, I hid under a shrub playing hide and seek and suddenly felt some living thing move under my foot. My heart almost stopped with terror, but it was only a fat old toad, the kind that sometimes hid under dead leaves or under the geranium plants.

Another time, we were playing in the Big Yard when, lying on the ground, not far from the woodpile, we found a small dead bird. We couldn't let that poor little creature just lie there. We had to have a funeral. We laid the body of the deceased in the coffin, a shoe box we'd found in the cellar, carefully padded with cotton and lined with silky cloth. We dug the grave in the orchard near the fence, where red Virginia creeper grew. We did our best to approximate the flower-heaped coffin, the sad-sounding music, the prayers for the dead, the holy water sprinkled on the coffin, the slow-moving procession to the grave site. We lowered the coffin into the grave and covered it with earth. After strewing the mound with violets and baby roses, we made a cross of two sticks to place at its head. We were glad that the kitchen windows looked out on the site, for we didn't want the poor little bird to be lonely, and we wanted to remember where he lay.

Our farm was a source of inexhaustible interest to Ev and me. In the fall, after the visiting threshers had removed the grain from the hay, a long pipe blew the straw residue out in a dusty cloud that formed a big stack. Once the work was done and the men had left, Ev and I ran to slide down that stack. Once was enough, however, for the itchy straw got down our backs and then we couldn't wait to get out of our clothes.

One year Papa grew a lot of pumpkins between the orchard trees, intending to break them up and feed them to the pigs. We liked to try to trap a bumblebee inside the long orange pumpkin flowers. Gingerly, we'd grasp the top of the blossom and try to shut it in before it could escape. Trapped bees made a very nice "buzzy-wuzzy" sound. Or we would catch them with our "clappers," two sticks made from split shingles. This was an exciting sport because it involved the danger of being stung. I was always rather queasy about any kind of "bee," since the time I stepped barefoot on a yellow jacket in my mother's bedroom. When the pumpkins got ripe, they were in unusual colors that I had never before seen in pumpkins—not bright orange but lovely soft pastel tones of blue-green, yellow, cream and orange. They weren't small either: some were as large as two feet in diameter. We were allowed to carve as many jack-o-lanterns as we wished.

We loved to see the baby chickens hatch, one by one pecking their way out of the shells, and we loved to cuddle their soft, velvety bodies in our two hands. We delighted in baby animals of all kinds. Baby colts, calves, even piglets with their flat, pushed-back noses, were all adorable. It was great fun to watch a row of calves drinking milk from a shallow trough, their tails waving rapidly back and forth in delight.

None of us children were afraid of horses. We thought of them as our friends, called them by name, and liked to pet them. Though they were very tame, we were always admonished to speak to them as we came near them. We found that a pat on the haunch beforehand would tell them who was there so they wouldn't be taken by surprise. Otherwise we might meet the same fate as that small child of Pa's first family who was kicked by a horse and died.

Sometimes Ev and I were given the task of taking them to the watering trough. Papa taught us to secure them with an easy-to-tie slip knot when we returned them to the stalls. A bowline (non-slip) knot was used for some things but not for this. We all learned to ride at an early age and to saddle up Nelly, the riding horse. There was nothing I loved better than galloping across the hilltops with the wind in my face and hair!

We weren't frightened of our cows and pigs, either. What Ev and I did fear was the big, red bull that was sometimes locked up in the bull pen next to the horse barn. It wasn't only that Papa had warned us to stay away from him, or that he had surrounded the pen with a very high fence of extra-heavy lumber; we just knew that that big old bull was as mean as mean could be. We were sure he was itching to get at us. The massive head, the thick muscular neck, the huge hunched-up shoulders might scare even a grownup. We were small and petrified (though it was also kind of fun to be scared). We would sneak up to take a quick look through the bars and then jump back in delicious alarm. "Watch out! He's headed our way!" we would cry, and then scurry back to the safety and warmth of Mama's kitchen.

In the winter and early spring, before the creek dried up, we would make expeditions up the gully to our treasured waterfall. Sometimes on the way back we would pick a variegated bouquet to take home to Mama—a handful of blue lupines, the wild flower that, with wild California poppies, gave us the state colors of blue and gold, or some purplish wild flax or scarlet pimpernel or gleaming yellow buttercups. We never failed to hold a buttercup up to each other's chin, looking for the yellow reflection that meant you liked butter.

On the walk home from school we used to dawdle along. We had a lot of fun catching the small green or yellow frogs in the water-filled ditch at the side of the road. Once this led to disaster. We filled a can with the tiny creatures and pushed the tin lid down to keep them in. Alas, we forgot to pick them up on the way home from school and much later we found them where we had left them, all dead. The memory of those lifeless little bodies haunted me for a long time.

Sometimes we'd see long, hairlike worms in the mud puddles. We had been told by bigger kids that a hair dropped from a horse's tail would turn into one of these. We had to grow

Evelyn and Rose in Sunday dresses, 1917. Ages 10 and 12.

much older before we discarded this idea of spontaneous generation.

Evelyn and I spent so much of our time together that we even invented some of our own private words. Lupine flowers were "biddy-widdies"; the dark brown, chocolate-like powder that came out of the small fungus puffballs we called "peprous-poutris," anything tiny was a "beegie," if your leg went to sleep and you couldn't stand on it, it was "all brittery," anything that smelled bad was "oofy," while vomit was "gomite," a word invented by our older sister Louise, which was a humorous adaptation of the Portuguese word, *"vomito."*

Our brother Tiny was a major source of the diversion in our lives. Once, having found a good piece of rope, he got a board and made a swing for Ev and me, hanging it from the old walnut tree. That swing gave us a lot of pleasure. He also made a narrow, flat bat with a shaped handle so we could all play baseball and I formed the ball out of old socks very tightly wrapped with string. Often in the soft light of summer evenings, we kids would play baseball out in the Big Yard.

Once Tiny trapped a ferret, which he put into a huge old metal drum so we could watch it run around. Somehow it managed to escape and was never seen again. Mama was annoyed for she feared it would kill her chickens. Then for a time we had a raccoon which he had caught and kept as a pet. Nadine, my little niece, Joe's daughter, doted on it. Gutsy kid that she was, she wouldn't let go even when it scratched the devil out of her arms.

Tiny made us a marvelous coaster from an old buggy that had seen better days. He removed the top and the shafts, then took a length of rope and tied each end of it to the axle near a front wheel, making a convenient loop to steer with. In front of our house a flat stretch of the graveled county road reached as far as the horse barn, with a hill at either end. Almost never did a car come by on that road in those early days and only rarely a buggy. Tiny would pull the coaster up to the top of the bigger hill, the one nearest the house, called Peters' Hill on local maps. Whoever was brave enough could get in and ride with him. Then he started us off and away we went, pigtails flying, down the hill for a breathtaking ride. Once our rig got going it never stopped until it was part way up the hill beyond the barn. It was more thrilling than a roller coaster.

But my older brothers mostly went off on their own, ignoring us girls. They were more than willing to sleep in the bunkhouse, not only because the main house was short on space, but because it gave them freedom to come and go on their bicycles, especially at night when Papa was already in bed. I never learned where they went or what they did except that I know Tiny used to go to dances at the San Ramon Hall every Saturday night.

Sometimes on hot summer days my brothers would go swimming in the abandoned reservoir for the town of Danville that remained on our ranch. It was a round concrete structure some thirty-five feet in diameter and someone had built a small wooden platform on one side, so it made a fine swimming pool. I'll bet my father never knew anything about it, as the reservoir was deep, and he would have thought it dangerous, not to mention a waste of time. We girls wouldn't have dared to do such a thing. We had never been swimming in our lives but even if we had known how to swim, we knew our father would consider it immodest behavior, unsuitable for girls.

On two memorable days, a year or two apart, Papa took Ma, Ev and me to Portuguese Holy Ghost festivals in Hayward. Those were the only times I remember using our surrey with the fringe on the top. It was pulled by May and Lena, a pair of our powerful draft horses that made a handsome buff-colored team, though they did seem a bit overgrown for the vehicle. On one of those days we had a picnic with my godmother and godfather, Mr. and Mrs. Manuel Lawrence, who were not related to my mother. We had soda pop, something new that I really liked, the bottle sealed with a wire clamp on a rubber-tipped stopper. Mrs. Lawrence gave me some olives, which were also new to me and which I didn't like at all. I was embarrassed to say so, so I held them in my hand until I could furtively stuff them up my elastic-bound bloomer legs. Speaking of my godmother, I am reminded that when I was very small, I was trained to touch my fingers to my lips and say, *"A bença, Madrinha"* whenever I saw her. I had no idea what I was saying but I now know it was, "Your blessing, Godmother."

The "Holy Ghost" was, and still is, the most important Azorean Portuguese festival of the year. Dating from the original settlement of the islands in the 15th century, the festivals continued to thrive in the Azores long after they had died out in the mother country. They honor the Holy Spirit, the third aspect of the Trinity, and the sainted Queen Isabel of Portugal, who distributed food to the poor. Associated with the Pentecost, they were celebrated primarily in the seven weeks following Easter. Every parish in the old country had a brotherhood of believers who organized the procession to the church, where their leader or a male child substitute was crowned "emperor" by the priest. Afterwards, in emulation of Queen Isabel, *sopas* (bread swimming in seasoned beef broth, with chunks of boiled beef) was given to all comers. Beef was a rare treat for the Azorean peasantry because, while they sometimes raised cattle for sale, they were too poor to eat them.

Azoreans brought their devotion to the Holy Ghost with them to the United States, but here there was a gradual transformation over the years, from a purely religious procession to a more Americanized parade. Before World War I, in the years I went to the *festas,* things were changing but were still relatively simple. A queen in her early teens was featured, replacing the old country's male emperor. Wearing a white gown and a tiara, she carried a crown topped with a dove, the symbol of the Holy Ghost, and marched within a square formed by four rods

Typical Holy Ghost festival of 1914. Pescadero, California. Courtesy Ron Duarte.

held together at the corners by four "side maids," also in white. She wore no elaborate cape as did later queens, nor did the parade include floats. At least one marching band played the Portuguese national anthem and other songs. Then came men carrying gold-fringed banners with the names of Portuguese brotherhoods such as the IDES *(Irmandade do Divino Espírito Santo),* which were established for mutual aid and charitable assistance, and the women of the SPRSI *(Sociedade Portuguesa Rainha Santa Isabel),* who fielded a drill team dressed in white. The *festas* became so popular that one was held somewhere in Northern California almost every weekend from Pentecost to September. I remember well those parades from my childhood though I must confess that it was the barrels of free lemonade put out for the kids that made the biggest impression on me.

Hayward's Holy Ghost parade always ended at the All Saints Church, where the queen was crowned and Mass was said. Afterward, *sopas* was distributed and there was folk dancing, including the circle dance called the *chamarita*. Hayward had no Holy Ghost bull fights although some other towns did, always "bloodless" fights in which the bull was not killed. Recently someone came up with a novel and amusing way to avoid causing pain to the animal when the banderillero plunges flagged darts into his hide—an expanse of velcro is wrapped around his shoulders and the darts are tipped with velcro so they will stick to it.

When I look back at my youth I think that I didn't miss much by having so few material possessions. Life on the farm was never dull. Without toys our imagination focused on the animals, the work going on, the natural world around us, and the few visitors we came into contact with. There was always something different to see and do. The one thing I do regret is the scarcity of books in my early life. I think that if Mama had had any idea how crucial reading is to learning and personal growth, she would have seen to it that we had books. But nothing in her life had taught her that, and we didn't know enough to ask.

Outsiders

EXCEPT FOR SCHOOL, church, and shopping trips to Danville or to Hayward for shoes, we girls almost never left the ranch. We knew little of the outside world. Our few excursions were therefore memorable, and so were the people who came to our home for one reason or another.

Most of our older brothers and sisters came to see us occasionally at times other than Thanksgiving and Christmas. While these visits were welcome, even exciting, we almost never visited any of them in return. Once, though, when I was very small, before we had the Buick, Papa decided to visit our jolly, good-natured sister Annie Lemos, who lived farthest away and could come to us only at holiday time. He hired a garage man to drive him, Ma, Evelyn and me to her family's home in Ripon in the San Joaquin Valley. I remember only two details of that visit; the house was situated in the middle of a field where a flock of crows was flying about, and Annie had a pincushion embroidered with some very lifelike red strawberries.

Another time we went to visit Mary Cabral, the eldest half-sister who had been burdened with housekeeping and the care of her younger siblings after their mother died. Mary was the poorest of our family. I was shocked that she and her husband Joe and their two children, Alfred and Madelyn, lived in a rented shack with only board and batten sheathing, no interior walls. But small, wiry Mary was a demon worker; that tiny house was scrubbed spotless and their few possessions were lined up in soldierly order. Somewhat later, Papa gave her, and the six other children of his first family, money that most of them used for housing. Mary and Joe built a small house on the southern outskirts of Danville.

The other farms in our immediate vicinity were owned by John and Elmer Baldwin, Bill Meese, the Cox family, George Oswill and Big John Bettencourt. We children had little contact with these families and none at all with their male members. We did know the Oswills because Thelma and Virginia Oswill were our classmates and, though we were supposed to come straight home from school, Ev and I would occasionally stop off at their house for a few minutes, tempted by the slide on their front veranda. Mrs. Oswill gave us leftover baking powder biscuits with delicious blackberry jam. They tasted especially good because what we got at home was mostly bland quince jelly that Mama made from the fruit of the quince tree by the cellar door. The girls' grandmother, who was always called "Old Lady Oswill" to differentiate her from their mother, was the mid-wife who had delivered us both, at home, and possibly some of my brothers, too.

Once when Ev and I were perhaps ten and twelve years old, we took it upon ourselves for some reason to pay a visit to a neighbor on the adjacent farm, Mrs. Meese, the grandmother of ex-Attorney General Ed Meese. The kindly old lady invited us into her parlor—I remember a rocking chair with her shawl draped over the back, a rag rug and lots of tidies here and

San Ramon Valley neighbors, 1910: Elworthy and Elmer Baldwin houses, foreground;
John Baldwin house in distance.

there—and chatted with us in a friendly, sociable way, almost as if we were grownups. She told us all about the firefall that she and her son Bill had seen on a recent vacation trip to Yosemite. A great stack of wood was constructed all along the edge of a tremendously high cliff, then set afire. When the wood had burned down to glowing embers, at a given signal a crew took rakes and pushed the fiery mass over the edge in a spectacular firefall. A large crowd in the meadow below thrilled at the sight. We were awed by this, as well as by her story of a redwood tree so huge that when a passageway was cut through the trunk a team of horses could be driven through it.

I marveled that Mr. Meese would take time off from his

farm work, even to go on such an interesting vacation. The very concept of a vacation was foreign to our family. Papa would never have done anything like that. His work was both his livelihood and his recreation; it was his life.

The neighbors our family knew best were Mr. and Mrs. Big John Bettencourt, though I don't remember that either of them ever came to our house. Papa gave him the nickname because he knew so many Portuguese men named John that he had to distinguish one from the other. In the typical way of the old country, he would give them names reflecting some prominent characteristic. One was *"o João dos olhos verdes,"* the John of the green eyes, or green-eyed John; another was *"o João das abóboras,"* John of the pumpkins. And Mr. Bettencourt was called *"o João grande,"* or Big John. Once assigned, the name stuck forever. He was indeed a big man, especially next to all of us short Peters's. Tall, gaunt, rawboned in appearance, he looked like the illustrations of Don Quixote I have seen in Spanish classes. His wife, known as "Mrs. Big John," was what I would later describe as a real Tugboat Annie type, and I'm ashamed of it for she couldn't have been kinder to us. She was a tall, rugged farm woman, a bit overweight, her hair in a straggly knot on top of her head. She wore a big, heavy pair of men's work shoes as she sloshed around in the mud of the cow corral. The two of them were childless, worked hard, lived poor, and owned next to nothing.

Once Mrs. Big John gave Mama a couple of sacks of Jonathan apples from her orchard to bring home to the family, and how we children did enjoy them! Every day after school I would eat all I could hold. After that, Mama, Ev and I sometimes went there to buy more. To this day Jonathans are my favorite apples.

Mrs. Big John lived an isolated life but she loved company, so Tiny used to telephone her every once in a while to tell her the latest news. She'd regularly answer in disbelief, saying "Wha? Wha?," so of course Tiny nicknamed her "Wa Wa," though not to her face.

I remember that someone found one of Big John's horses dead, its head all tangled up in a barbed wire fence. Frank, or maybe it was Joe, joked that Big John worked his horse so hard for such long hours and fed it so little that the unhappy nag had committed suicide. I always picture that horse as Don Quixote's Rosinante.

Mama told me that Mr. and Mrs. Big John had inadvertently caused Pa a lot of chagrin and disappointment. He had heard that the Oswill family ranch was for sale, a good property with some choice flat land that bordered our home ranch and extended south all the way to the San Ramon School. Land-hungry Papa really wanted it, but he was reluctant to pay the asking price. Mama advised him to buy it but he wanted to hold off for a while in case the owners would take less. "Who else could come up with that kind of money?" he asked.

Big John Bettencourt could and did. The Bettencourt property also bordered the Oswill ranch, on the western, Bollinger Canyon side, and it was this man who beat out my father in the competition for the Oswill place. I think my father learned some valuable lessons from this experience: One, if it's worth it and you really want it, buy it. Don't try for a lower price. Two, don't judge by appearances. A man may look poor but, especially if he's a Portuguese immigrant, his style of living can deceive you. In any case, Pa later told Mama,

"You gave me *boms conselhos* (good advice)." This was a rare admission for him to make since he had great confidence in his own shrewdness and ability to make the right decisions.

Some of the people who came to our house were strangers, who fascinated me as a child. One of my very early memories is of a man leading a cattle drive up the road, remarkable as this may seem in Contra Costa County. His cattle, a weird lot in my eyes, were strangely different from our short-horned red and white Herefords. Huge and raw-boned, their wide and lofty horns gave them an alien look. I can still hear their bellowing and see them milling about and tossing their heads as they feinted and jousted with each other. Where they came from or where they were going I never knew; I was too young to think of asking. In any case, my father put them up in the Big Yard where a traveling herd could be safe. I doubt that he took any payment, as it wasn't his custom to charge for such favors.

But as it happens, there was one reward. A calf was born to one of the cows during the night. The poor thing's front feet were bent backwards at the dewclaw just above the hoof and it was unable to travel with the herd. It was left behind as a gift for my father, who gave it to Ev and me. Never a pet, the calf was cared for with the rest of the herd after its feet straightened out of their own accord. Likewise, it was sold with them when the time came and the proceeds started our first bank account. Later it would form the nucleus of a college expense fund.

Another time, also when I was small, an old Portuguese man whom I had never seen before came to see Papa. He wasn't at home and the stranger opted to sit on the front porch to wait for him. Before long he took off one of his shoes and slowly unwrapped a long strip of cloth from around his foot and ankle. He then carefully rewrapped the foot to his satisfaction and replaced the shoe, only to do the same with the other foot. I thought that he was probably too poor to buy socks. I have since heard that foot-wrapping used to be a common practice in the pre-Revolutionary Azores—that is, before the overthrow of the Salazar dictatorship in 1974. When I visited the islands for the first and only time in 1992, Rosa, a distant cousin some twenty years younger than I, told me that shoes were luxuries when she was growing up. Many people went barefoot; luckily it is a mild, if damp, climate and never gets near freezing. She told me laughingly that her brother bought his first pair of shoes at age eighteen to go to a dance, hoping to impress a girl, but they pinched his feet so badly that he had to walk home with them slung over his shoulder.

In 1917, when I was in the seventh grade, the United States entered World War I. Shortly thereafter, Mary and Mira More, unmarried sisters who, though middle-aged, were always known as "the More girls," came to our house. As their contribution to the war effort, they were going around the area teaching grade schoolers to knit. We girls would knit wool strips of alternating pink and blue squares which were later sewed together to make "Blankets for Belgian Babies." The boys used thick wooden needles to knit strips of cotton material for use as mop rags. We kids also saved tinfoil, and we gathered black walnuts because we were told they would be used in making gas masks. Everyone was asked to save white flour for "Our Boys," so Mama baked rye and corn breads for the family. As a food conservation measure, several government inspectors taught local farmers to poison the ground squirrels that ate so much wheat. My father learned to make balls of sacking, saturate them with carbon bisulfide, poke them into the squirrel burrows, then stop up the entrances with dirt. Many were killed in this way, though some survived, and it did lead to a small increase in the yield per acre.

Everyone was very patriotic. Danville held parades with flag-waving kids piled into trucks, singing *Over There,* and there was a fashion among young women for wearing khaki dresses. My half-brothers were too old to go as soldiers, my brothers too young. But two of my cousins went, sons of Mama's sisters, Mary Freitas and Louise Bettencourt. They later came home safely. In all, the war didn't have a lot of impact on the lives of us kids on the ranch and we had no idea at all what the political issues were or why we were fighting.

The other visitors were the tradesmen, peddlers and laborers who came to the house to sell their goods and services. The meat, fish and vegetable men visited us weekly. One woman regularly walked the entire four miles from Danville carrying a huge nesting basket that must have weighed fifty pounds. The two halves, one of which fitted over the other, were held together by a heavy strap. She would take them apart on our kitchen floor to display her wares, which included sewing notions like needles, pins, safety pins, buttons, rick-rack, thimbles and darning cotton; personal items like hair pins, combs and shoelaces; almost anything saleable that wasn't heavy to carry. Mama would always buy something whether she needed it or not because that poor woman had such a hard way to make a living. I think now she may have been one of the itinerant Jewish peddlers that I have read were widespread in the early days of Jewish immigration.

A tinsmith came by and mended tin pans for Mama. He had a soldering iron and a small furnace-like device to heat it with. Tin pans were in common use at the time, but with the farms so far apart, his must have been a poor living.

The Watkins man made regular calls. From him Mama would buy a big bottle of vanilla and a highly touted liniment that she sometimes used on her lame hip. A five inch can of Carbo salve was also a must—said to contain carbolic acid, guaranteed to work as well for horses' galled shoulders as for our own cuts and bruises. Like the liniment, it had a powerful smell that was most reassuring. Once, however, Ma made the mistake of buying a small can of expensive stain remover for clothing that turned out to be nothing more than jellied soap.

A couple of black men came by one day looking for work and Papa hired them to whitewash the horse barn. They were the first black people I had seen, and the only ones I would ever see until age 18 when I left the ranch for the university. When I asked Pa why their faces were black he pointed to a package of lampblack on the washhouse shelf and said, with a twinkle in his eye, "They must have used some of that." It was the only answer I ever got, and I was puzzled because he seemed to be joking.

Now and then a chicken man would come to buy a few of Mama's chickens. He would pack them in with others in a coop in the back of his wagon. "Aren't you afraid they'll die?" Mama asked. "Sometimes they do," he replied, "But they're good enough for tamales."

An old guy named Toomey used to come and offer to mend our harness, and one day I saw him sprawled against the Big Yard fence. Tiny said he was drunk. As I didn't even know

Joe Peters' sister, Maria Josefa Rosa, in old age, 1931. Beira, São Jorge Island, Azores.

the meaning of the word, he explained that when people drink too much alcohol they can't walk or talk properly. I thought that was a bad way to be. We never had any liquor in our house, not even the wine that most Portuguese drink in moderation, as Pa had had a bad experience with alcohol when he was a teenager. After drinking too much wine he played a practical joke on an old lady he knew: "Which is better?" he asked her, "A little or a lot?" "Well," she said, "A lot is usually better than a little." "So take a lot then," he replied, hitting her lightly with a stick he was carrying. Under the influence of alcohol it had seemed funny, but he was so heartily ashamed of himself when he sobered up that he determined never to drink again. And he didn't. Once, though, someone—perhaps one of Papa's sisters in the Azores—sent us a bottle of port wine and Frances let me take a sip. It was a bit strange but I liked it because it was so sweet.

These seemingly insignificant incidents were important to me as a child and, given my relative isolation and the scantiness of my experience, they stimulated my imagination. They are mostly pleasant memories and I enjoy looking back at them. However, I also remember times when illness and death cast their shadows over me and my family.

Death and Sickness

EVEN AS SMALL CHILDREN, Ev and I went to funerals with our parents. It was our custom, and in any case they never hired a baby sitter in their lives, had probably never even heard of one. In those days more people died at an early age, and Mama came from a big family, so there were occasional funerals to go to. I doubt that it ever occurred to my parents that there was anything wrong with taking the children, and I think they were right. They knew that sooner or later we'd have to confront the fact that death is inevitable.

Mama told me once that in her youth when someone died, before funeral parlors became common, the family would wash the body and lay it out on a door that had been removed for that purpose while waiting for the coffin. They would place pennies on the eyes to keep them shut until rigor mortis had fixed them closed.

However, by the time I came along, the family and friends usually met at the funeral parlor the day before the funeral to say the rosary. On the day of the mass and funeral each person went up to the open casket to pay respects and see the deceased for the last time, then knelt by the casket to say a prayer. After that the casket was removed from the church to a hearse and the procession followed by horse and buggy to the gravesite, where final prayers were said. Somebody threw in a handful of soil and then the grave was filled in.

Whenever the family received a letter edged in black my parents opened it with dread and trepidation. I remember seeing one such letter when I was very young, probably announcing the death of one of Papa's two sisters back in Beira. Except for John Soares and two other nephews, Manuel and John Furtado, who emigrated to the United States, Papa would never again see any of the family he left behind at eighteen.

One day, Ev and I saw what we called "the dead wagon" (a hearse) pass by on the road in front of our house. There was nothing at all about it to mar the effect of total blackness: the coach was black, the driver's uniform was black, even the coats of the two fine horses were as velvety black as the darkest night. Though the dead wagon had wide glass windows on either side, they were framed by curtains of heavy black velvet, luxuriously fringed and tasseled and drawn back to the sides so that one could catch a glimpse of the coffin inside. We were awed at the sight.

In those days, people had a lot more grandeur in death than they ever had in life. Even the poorest people we knew seemed somehow to provide a dignified last ride for their loved ones. Certainly there wasn't a lot they could do for them while they were sick, for medical care as we know it today was almost non-existent when I was growing up. Families were large, the germ theory remained unknown to most people, and professional care was not easily available. In later years there was a doctor in Danville but very seldom did he arrive at our farm with his little black bag of medicines.

For minor problems, Mama usually relied on folk remedies. For chest colds she used mustard plasters, for coughs a mixture of honey and lemon juice, for upset stomachs an unlikely soup of fried onions, water and vinegar. Whether or not these worked, it comforted us to feel that something was being done. Sometimes my family resorted to superstitions from the old country. For example, when Mama thought my hair was too thin, she cut off a lock, wrapped a string around it and tied it to the branch of a young tree. The idea was that as the tree grew stronger and thicker, so would my hair. For a persistent nosebleed my older sister Louise once recommended putting a knife under the mattress to "cut" the flow of blood.

Before penicillin, infectious diseases were common killers. Pneumonia took both my maternal grandfather and Papa's first wife, and in the 1930's it nearly killed both Mama and Papa at once, though they both pulled through eventually. Tuberculosis, "consumption" as it was called, was a scourge. Grownups spoke of it with fear in their voices, which was communicated to us children. If several members of a family died of it, that family became known as a "consumption family." It touched us, too, for Lizzie, my brother Frank's first wife, whom I liked, died of the disease.

Because my brother Joe's wife, Adeline, came down with typhoid fever during her pregnancy, their daughter Nadine was born prematurely. Desperate, Joe came to Mama for help. She offered to care for the baby, saying she would do her best to save it, but that Joe must not hold it against her if she failed. Mama used to say that Nadine was so tiny that a man's handkerchief folded in fourths could serve as a diaper. Mama wrapped her up, placed her in a shoe box, and kept warmed

Nadine Peters at 12 years, 1925.

bricks around the box as a kind of improvised incubator. The baby was bottle-fed but was too weak to suckle for long, so a nipple had to be kept in her mouth almost constantly. Mama, patient and persevering, managed to pull her through, probably with Frances's help as the oldest girl at home. I remember that later she used to feed Nadine something called Mellin's Food, which looked like malted milk but may have been some sort of cereal that was added to milk. She stayed with us for quite some time and when she finally went home to her mother she was plump and thriving. Both Adeline and Joe always felt that they could never repay what Mama had done for them. In later years, when she was old, they were conscientious about coming to visit her regularly.

Midwives delivered babies at home in those days. Prenatal

care and pediatric medicine were unheard of. The death of children was common. Mama had lost Little Louie from diarrhea and a child from Papa's first family had been killed by a horse. Still, the survival of twelve out of a family of fourteen children was then a good record. Measles, mumps, chicken pox and whooping cough swept through periodically and once there was an epidemic of diphtheria in Danville in which at least one girl died. There were no childhood inoculations, or at least I never heard of any, and there were none in my schools. Recently a doctor couldn't believe that I had never in my life had a diphtheria or tetanus shot. "Oh," she said, "You must have!" In fact, the only disease I was ever vaccinated against was smallpox when I entered the university.

My oldest sister Mary and her husband Joe Cabral had the misfortune to lose a child at birth. Burial in the Catholic graveyard was denied to them because the child had not been baptized, so Joe dug a grave and the heartbroken parents laid the baby to rest in their own backyard. Mary was proud and hot-tempered. She could not understand how their own church could do this to them. As if the pain of losing their child weren't enough! To the best of my knowledge, she never set foot in church again.

When Ed was in third grade he almost died as the result of a ruptured appendix. Brother Frank was the first one to realize the danger and warned my parents that he was near death. They took him to Dr. Coleman at Merritt Hospital in Oakland. When he was recovering from the operation, day after day my mother would hitch up the horse to the buggy and drive the many miles to visit him. Some people were "fresh air fiends" in those days—open-air sleeping porches were all the rage—and, though Ed was critically ill, his nurse insisted on letting a blast of cold air blow in directly on him. Mama finally set her foot down and told her she had better not open that window again. I think she felt that with her experience she knew more about caring for children than that young sprout of a nurse.

One day Ed was allowed to come home from the hospital, wearing a bandage around his abdomen. In the morning my parents went in to check on him. They were aghast when they removed the bandage and discovered that the wound had leaked infected material into the abdominal cavity, causing the incision to burst open and release a quantity of foul-smelling pus. I was standing in the doorway, waiting to learn how Ed was doing. Papa was a man who didn't readily show his feelings, yet I never will forget the groan of anguish that escaped his lips at the sickening sight.

Ed was returned to the hospital and although he recovered, our local doctor warned Papa that he'd never be strong enough to do heavy farm labor. Since he was a good student they decided he should get more education to prepare him for some other job. This was the reason that Ed happened to be the first of the family not only to graduate from high school but to be sent on to the University of California. Nothing in Papa's or Mama's experience had taught them the value of higher education, and Papa probably felt that prolonged schooling was a waste of one's best working years. The doctor was wrong about Ed's health, for he recovered fully, but the error did get him an education and, indirectly, prepared the way for first me and then Evelyn to follow in his footsteps.

A great many people lost their lives during the great flu

epidemic of 1918. We were instructed in school to wear gauze masks in the hope of warding off the disease. That did our family no good; all nine of us came down with it. Either we were remarkably strong or we didn't have the most severe form, because it seemed to us only a little worse than the usual flu, with its fever, cough, and aches and pains. We had no idea that millions of people worldwide were dying of it. Fortunately, dear, kind Mrs. Penn, a nurse from Danville, took charge of cooking, feeding and sponge baths. She pulled us all through. I remember my father paying her at least once with a huge, shining gold piece which he fished from a small leather sack he carried in his pocket. My mother gave her a handsome square scarf which Papa's sister had sent from the Azores. Nothing would have been too good for her.

However, our family did not escape tragedy altogether. About 1911, when my brother Manuel was twenty-two, a horse he was riding near Dublin shied at something and broke away from the road, running at full speed into a hop yard. At that point the hops were trained up a tall trellis, from which a guy wire slanted down to the ground. The frightened horse dashed wildly under the wire. Manuel could not duck in time; the wire caught him across the neck and threw him to the ground.

His throat was not cut, he could speak normally and was not disfigured, but the function of his throat was terribly damaged. One local doctor thought it was mainly nerve damage. Another disagreed. But whatever the cause, Manuel was no longer able to swallow anything, not even a drop of water. Although it seemed hopeless, Papa was unwilling to give up. Someone told him that the Mayo Brothers' Clinic had the best doctors in the United States and so he sent Manuel by train to Minnesota, in the care of a friend, to be examined there. But they could do nothing for him.

When he left the clinic, the doctor gave him a little box filled with sawdust that he could carry with him to dispose of saliva or phlegm, since he couldn't swallow them either, though I never saw him use it. For the rest of his life Manuel would have to take all nourishment—liquid, of course— through a funnel attached to the upper end of a tube that he thrust all the way down into his stomach. He learned to do this for himself without much gagging. Mama prepared his food— soups and eggnogs, anything that could be made liquid enough to run down the tube.

After his accident Manuel came back to live on the farm. I'm sure Papa didn't allow him to do farm work, for no one could do heavy labor on that limited diet. For the rest of his life he stayed at home where his stepmother could prepare his food for him. He didn't lose weight but he would often sit in the kitchen, still and silent, for long periods of time. He never married.

I never once heard him complain but he began to spend much of his time in the Danville pool hall, on Main Street just across from the Bank of Italy, where he played cards with friends. I think some people, including my father, thought it was not a very respectable place but Papa never said anything about it to Manuel. About fifteen years after the accident, when I was already married and living at a distance from home, I got word that he had died, choked to death while try- ing to eat an apple.

That wasn't a true story. I only learned recently from

Frank's daughter, Gertrude, what really caused his death. Our brother Frank was a partner in the Freitas and Peters Store, a general merchandise store on Main Street. One day someone came running in from the nearby pool hall to tell him that Manuel had died there. Apparently he had acquired the habit of pouring whiskey down his feeding tube, and he had taken a fatal amount. While it may or may not have been accidental, the apple-choking story must have been a cover-up. Suicide would have precluded his burial in a Catholic cemetery and even if the death were accidental, to die drinking whiskey in a poolroom would have shamed the family.

After his death, there was a surprising development. It seems that Manuel was holding title in his name to some property that had been paid for by a Japanese immigrant. No Asian-born person could legally own property in California at that time, nor could they apply for citizenship, so unless they had American-born children, in order to buy any property they had to find a citizen they trusted to hold the land for them. Title would have passed to Papa after Manuel's death. While he would never have taken something that didn't belong to him and certainly would have honored Manuel's promises, I never heard how the matter was settled.

Most of the time my parents enjoyed fairly good health. Although Papa wore heavy woolen underwear in winter, he sometimes came down with severe chest colds anyway. (I know that doctors now say that inclement weather has nothing to do with colds, but I'm not convinced.) Then Mama would apply the standard home remedy of the time, a mustard-plaster poultice. She made a paste of dry mustard and water and spread it between two squares of muslin. This she would apply to Papa's chest for as long as he could stand it, for the plaster burned and stung. Impatient to get well so he could get back to work and thinking more would be better, he would always order her to "Leave it on till it blist!"

Because Ma suffered from "stomach problems" she was always dosing herself with castor oil, Pluto Water and Garfield Tea, all laxatives or what she called "physics," and various pills prescribed by Doctor Michael. At times she also used Chinese herbs. I don't know how she heard about them, but she was always on the lookout for anything that would help her chronic stomach pain. At ninety she told me that many years earlier, while driving to town, she experienced such pain that she had to stop the buggy and lie down in the grass by the side of the road. Some of the family suspected that she was something of a hypochondriac, but years later another doctor diagnosed a hiatal hernia, where part of the stomach wall protrudes upward through the diaphragm.

In addition, Mama always walked with a marked limp even though Mr. Thorup, the San Ramon shoemaker, built up the heel of her right shoe a couple of inches to compensate for her short leg. Sometimes it pained her but she seldom complained and never seemed to consider herself a cripple. She almost always ignored the problem and therefore it did not exist. Always cheerful, she went about her work just like any other farm woman with a normal stomach and two good, sound legs.

Expanding Horizons

IN 1919, I ENROLLED at Danville's San Ramon Valley
Union High School, two weeks late and only after my parents
received a notice that they were required by law to send me. A
measure requiring compulsory attendance to age sixteen had
just been enacted. As law-abiding citizens, they complied, but
they obviously thought it was a waste of time to send a daughter to school since girls would just get married soon and start
raising a family. I had always liked school and was very unhappy that I was expected to stay home and help Mama with the
household chores forever, especially while my brother Ed was
allowed to go on to high school. I was hoping that when my
kind-hearted mother understood how much it meant to me, I
could convince her to let me go, too. Then the letter from the
school board arrived. I was very thankful for compulsory education.

Danville was then a small town, little more than a village.
Its three primary streets were sandwiched between the
Oakland, Antioch and Eastern Railroad (the O.A.and E.) and
San Ramon Creek. Only a few places of business lined Hartz
Avenue, the main street. One was the San Ramon Valley Bank
(later the Bank of Italy), where my father always did his

Freitas and Peters Big Store parade float, "Our Picnic." Danville, May 1920.

banking, a very small building by today's standards. Behind the bank and opening onto the side street was Joe Lawrence's butcher shop. Next to the bank was the Freitas and Peters Store, owned by my oldest brother Frank and his partner, which sold not only fruits, vegetables and groceries but sundries and a limited choice of yardage for clothing. On the other side of the street were the barbershop; the drugstore with its soda fountain, where once in a long while Ma would treat me to an ice cream cone; and the pool hall my brother Manuel frequented. It had been Elliott's Bar until 1919 when Prohibition made selling liquor illegal.

St. Isidore Catholic Church, where all the family attended Mass on Sundays, was located farther down Hartz Avenue in the direction of Alamo. My mother was a deeply religious woman although she didn't talk much about it until she became very old. Perhaps she was too busy when we kids were

Motorcyclists ready for parade in front of Freitas and Peters store, Hartz Ave., Danville, May, 1920. Tiny third from left.

at home. My father never talked about religion at all, but like most people he was faithful to the church he was raised in. As for me, I had dutifully learned the catechism by rote as a small child. But in church, though I tried to be quiet and well-behaved, I found it hard to sit through the long passages of unintelligible Latin. Luckily, parables such as the multiplication of the loaves and fishes, the Good Samaritan, and the cleansing of the lepers were narrated in English, and these held my interest. Usually, however, I would while away the time by making a careful study of the attire and mien of all the religious statues. When the possibilities of that diversion were exhausted I would turn my attention to the religious paraphernalia on and above the altar. As a last resort I would make a study of the cracks and brownish water stains on the once-white ceiling; I think I learned all their sizes and shapes by heart. Later, when I left home, I ended my connection with the Catholic Church, or any religion. I have never understood the belief in the supernatural.

Past the church, perhaps a quarter of a mile farther along what had by then become a paved highway, was the high school. The O. A. and E. railroad ran along next to the highway, its operation informal enough that a teacher who commuted to work by train would sometimes be dropped off in front of the school instead of at the station.

In Danville proper, Railroad Avenue paralleled Hartz Avenue. The tracks ran along one side and a few houses on the opposite, including those of my brother Frank and his children, and my sister Louise and her husband, George Lawrence. On Front Street, running along the creek on the other side of town, were the Oddfellows Hall, the Presbyterian Church, and the home office of our family dentist, Dr. Vecki, a white Gothic Revival style Victorian with a veranda extending across the front and lots of filigree wood trim. I worried about the huge wisteria with its mass of purple flowers that climbed up to the veranda roof and threatened to devour all the gingerbread. Across the creek from Dr. Vecki's office was another big white house that belonged to Mr. Flournoy, for whom my sister Frances worked. He was a man of many interests, who was employed by the railway, dealt in grain, feed, lumber and coal, and sold insurance from his home.

A wide bridge about 25 feet long and made of stout wooden planks crossed the deep San Ramon Creek, and from it a graveled road wandered away through fields and over gently rolling hills into the Tassajara Valley. It was in that valley that my maternal grandparents, Manuel and Mary Lawrence, had settled as pioneers. By the time I was in high school, five of their twelve children were rearing families on their own farms in the valley. My cousin Rose Ferreira told me that a street in the area still bears the Lawrence name.

Not long before I graduated from grammar school I had a traumatic experience when some nasty boy called me "Buck-rake Teeth." I guess I had known before that my teeth stuck out more than others' did but now I felt like a freak. You have to know what a buck-rake looked like to recognize the insult. It was an implement that was used to pull hay together into a shock, consisting of six or eight long, flat teeth attached at right angles to a back frame. I was so angry and miserable that I ran home to tell my mother, who was equally upset. Right away she sent me to Dr. Vecki to have my teeth straightened. Orthodontia was then a new and advanced procedure but Mama knew that he had already tried it once, straightening the protruding teeth of her friend Mrs. Norris's daughter.

I think the price was $100, a considerable sum in those days, but Mama didn't hesitate to spend it. I've always been grateful that she did that for me. For that matter, I don't think Papa objected to spending the money, either, or I would have heard something about it. Later, Dr. Vecki would straighten my sister Evelyn's teeth as well.

I have vivid memories of those sessions in the dentist chair. A ribbon of metal was cemented around each of the rear molars. Two adjustable wire bands stretching around the upper and lower sets of teeth were attached to the four molars, with a mechanism on each tooth for tightening the bands. But that wasn't all. Dr. Vecki wrapped a ribbon of metal around each of my front teeth, too. The ends of the ribbon strips came together in a ridge on the front surface of each tooth. The wire bands

Evelyn at sixteen, July 1923.

rested on these ridges.

Those sharp ridges cut into the sensitive tissues of my lips and caused me pain, as did the fine metal wires that the dentist wrapped around each individual tooth and twisted together in front. Though the ends of the wire were tucked under, there was no remedy for the resulting ridge. Sometimes the band from a molar would work loose from the tooth and dangle in my mouth for an entire weekend before it could be repaired. On the wall of the dentist's office was a picture of a smiling, freckle-faced, red haired kid with one front tooth missing. A caption underneath read, "It didn't hurt a bit." I used to look at it ruefully and think, "Well, maybe it didn't hurt *you*."

Ed (top right) and high school friends, 1920.

I never complained, though. I was so unhappy with my buck teeth that I would have put up with any amount of pain to get them straightened. I was grateful, too, to the enterprising Dr. Vecki. I think the whole process took about a year and was finished just before I entered high school. It did a lot for my self-confidence to enroll with straight teeth.

During my first year in high school, Ed, who was a year ahead of me, drove us both to school in the buggy pulled by old Lily. Later, Harry Hurst, San Ramon's storekeeper and postmaster, picked us up in his rattletrap truck, a makeshift school bus. My high school years were pleasant enough, but uneventful. I liked my teachers and did well in my studies, though I didn't find them exciting. The entire high school had fewer than 50 students. We certainly couldn't complain about lack of individual attention since there were only about four of us in most classes.

I took the usual courses in English and history, as well as algebra, geometry, general science, chemistry, typing and three years of Spanish. I especially enjoyed mechanical drawing and sewing, in which I already had considerable skill. I learned a lot of fancy embroidery stitches in the sewing class and made myself three cotton dresses: one in old rose crepe with a black running-stitch trim, and two plaid ginghams, one yellow and one pink.

Girls did not have physical education or organized team sports, although I once captained one of two pick-up baseball teams which competed at lunch time. Ed and most of the other boys were involved with the track and basketball teams, practicing after school to compete against other schools in Dublin, Pleasanton, Antioch, Brentwood, Crockett and Martinez. Since I had to catch the school bus home immediately after school was out, I had no part in any after-school activities like the school plays. However, I did all the illustrations for the yearbooks. I had always liked to draw and I must have been sensitive to visual images, for I can still vividly picture the wallpaper border in Dr. Vecki's office, which featured red-coated Englishmen and baying hounds engaged in a fox hunt. Perhaps such images were more striking because our home offered no visual stimulation whatever.

Ed, described as the resident "literary genius," was the yearbook editor for the class of 1922. In it he published two poems and I a story. Both of us demonstrated some fluency with words and good grammar skills but our writings were

Illustrations by Rose Peters for The Valley Kernel, *1922, San Ramon Valley Union High School Yearbook.*

composed almost entirely of cliches. My own story, *Easy Money,* about a fur trader and an Indian, was patterned after the pulp westerns, crudely written magazines on cheap paper, that my brothers sometimes brought home in those years. Aside from schoolbooks, they constituted all of our available reading material, for there was no school library. I am embarrassed to admit that my Indian's statements all ended with "Ugh."

As for music, when we were very small, we used to beg Ma to sing us a little song, to the tune of *My Bonnie Lies Over the Ocean,* that she had learned in school:

My kitty has gone from her basket.
My kitty has gone up a tree.
Oh, who will go 'mongst the branches
And bring back my kitty to me?

For a long time that was pretty much the extent of music in our house. However, when I was a freshman, Mama, remembering how much she had enjoyed the music played at family dances when she was young, decided to buy a Victrola, a wooden box about four feet high with a lift-up, hinged lid and a wind-up crank at the side. A few oddly miscellaneous records came with it, including the *Marseillaise* (I learned all the French words although I had no idea what they meant); a jazzy dance piece then very popular that went "Ja da, ja da, ja da ja da jing jing jing"; and a soppy song called *Tell Mother I'll be There*:

Tell Mother I'll be there
In answer to her prayer.
I promised her before she died
For heaven to prepare.
Oh, tell my darling mother
I'll be there.

Another was a love song, *Let the Rest of the World Go By*:

With someone like you, a pal good and true,
I'd like to leave it all behind
And go and find
Some place that's known to God alone,
Just a spot to call our own.
We'll find perfect peace,

San Ramon Valley Union High School, October 1921. Second row: Evelyn eighth from left; Rose fourteenth from left. Third row: Ed third from left

Where joys never cease
And let the rest of the world go by.

Tiny bought a small, puppet-like stick figure that would dance a lively if jerky jig when he placed it on the spinning record, and I remember that Papa got a great kick out of this. There was still something of the child in that gruff personality.

My world expanded during my high school years. The most remarkable event was my first moving picture. Mama drove us to Oakland in the Buick to see *Hearts of the World,* a melodramatic story about World War I directed by D. W. Griffith and starring Lillian and Dorothy Gish. I was struck by the film's closing image, a lengthy close-up of a potted flower on a window sill, which I must have grasped was a symbol of peace. Only a grammar school excursion in 1915 to the San Francisco World's Fair had been as exciting. There I saw the wonderful Tower of Jewels, embedded with pieces of colored glass that did indeed shine like jewels before my dazzled eyes. That was also my first glimpse of San Francisco, the city that would later be my home. But commercial entertainments like movies and fairs were foreign to our way of life on the farm. During all my years at home, I set foot in a restaurant only once, when Tiny treated Ev and me to the blue-plate special at a cafe on a trip to Livermore.

Other girls at school had much more freedom than Evelyn and I did, being allowed to visit each other's homes and casually wander around the village. I picked up from them the concept of fashion in clothes and hairstyles. Fortunately, I never had to wear the long, draggy skirts that had so encumbered my mother and older sisters in their work on the ranch,

Rose Peters, 1922, age 17.

for skirt lengths rose to mid-calf after the war and were to get shorter still in the 1920's. I was pleased that the new dresses I made in sewing class resembled what my classmates were wearing.

For a while I wore my long hair in a popular style that required much back-combing over the ears and ended up looking as if the hair were smoothed over a pair of earmuffs. When bobbed hair became the rage in 1923, I didn't ask Papa for permission to cut mine because I knew his rigid ideas about propriety for women. Instead, taking my cue from Mama's way of managing him, I just did it. He only noticed it about a week later when I was sitting at the dinner table and then what could he do? It was a fait accompli. He complained to Mama, "Look what she went and done to her hair!" but she successfully smoothed things over, saying, "Her hair is too thin. Cutting it will make it grow in thicker."

I also escaped Pa's scrutiny when it came to dancing. Before we got the Victrola, Mama taught me to waltz on the linoleum floor of the kitchen while I hummed the music. I think she had loved to dance and I did too. At school during lunch hour (we brought bag lunches from home) we played a player piano in the assembly hall, and I would sometimes dance with one of the other girls. The only time I went to an official school dance was when I graduated, but several times in my senior year Tiny took me along to the regular Saturday night dances in the San Ramon Community Hall. I danced the waltz, the fox-trot and sometimes the polka to music from a Victrola, most often with Tiny's friends Nolie or Lee Norris. Once he took me to Ramona Park, a private park with an outdoor dance floor that was located across the road from our Home Ranch amidst the trees in Meese's Grove. Soda water ("pop") was sold in booths there, and during the day innocent activities like sock races provided fun for the youngsters.

Pa was already asleep when our excursions took place and I didn't tell him for fear he would forbid them. He was so rigid in his ways and we were so afraid of his anger that all of us (except maybe Evelyn, who believed in following the rules) learned that we had to sneak around behind his back if there was something we really wanted to do. When Frances was in her twenties she was still living at home and therefore, by Pa's standards, under his control. She went out to a dance and was just coming in the back door when she heard him getting up to go to the bathroom. Desperate to avoid confrontation, she

Entrance gate, Ramona Park.

raced to her bedroom and, though it had been raining hard, dived into bed without a second thought and pulled up the covers over mud-caked shoes, soaked coat and all.

When my high school graduation neared, Mama took me all the way to Hayward, where she bought me just about the prettiest dress I had ever seen. Made of heavy, white Canton silk crepe it was, with narrow rows of hand-rolled, self-fabric rose petals edging the sleeves and neck. It was simple and gracefully cut, with tapered, draped, bias-cut hip panels over-laying a straight skirt. I loved that dress because it made me feel so attractive and I loved my mother for buying something so expensive to make me happy.

My graduation in 1923 was a very special occasion for me

Sather Gate, University of California, Berkeley, 1923.

and the whole family, as no girl before me had gone to high school. Even Papa attended. I enjoyed it greatly though I did lament that I'd lost my chance to be valedictorian by getting a couple of poor grades in my first semester, because I entered two weeks late and then didn't get my books for two more weeks.

The doctor's belief that Ed's appendicitis attack had left him too weak to do farm work opened the way for him to go the University of California. By the time I graduated, he had been at Berkeley for a year. I told Mama that if he could go it was only fair that I should be allowed to go, too, explaining that I could work three or four hours a day for room and board as other Cal students were doing. She agreed, and through the University Placement Service I was able to find live-in housework with a professor of philosophy and his family. When I left for the university, at almost eighteen, it was the first time in my life that I had spent a night away from home.

Afterword

I'M NOT SURE of the date, but Pa was probably in his seventies when a derrick that he used for lifting hay fell on him and injured one of his legs. Despite Mama's urging he refused to go to a doctor. He thought it would get better with time as his injuries usually did, but later x-rays showed a badly healed fracture just below the hip joint. Thereafter his leg caused him pain and he walked with a cane for the rest of his long life. After the accident he could no longer ride horseback, so when he needed to check on the cattle Mama would drive him in their big, high-clearance Buick right up over the rough, steep hills of the pastures. Pa never learned to drive a car.

When my parents became too old to run the farm any longer and Pa developed an infection in his foot that wouldn't heal, Ma decided she wanted a small home that would be warm in winter and easy to clean. They rented out the ranch and built a house for themselves in Danville, next door to my sister Louise Lawrence's house on Railroad Avenue. Papa spent his last year there. He didn't complain about the move but he couldn't have been happy, for the ranch had been his entire life. In the new house he had nothing to do but sit on the front porch and watch what little activity took place on the street

Peters family reunion at roundup time, about 1933–34. Kneeling, left to right: Joe, Elwin Lemos, Howard Peters, Bob Johnson, Dolores Peters, Manuel Bettencourt, Ronald Peters, Frank. Standing: Manuel Lemos, Ed, Annie, Annie Bettencourt (Rose Peters' sister), Frances, Rose Peters, Joe Peters. On fence: Pearl Peters, Charlotte ?, Bettencourt child, Viva Denise Johnson, Gertrude Peters, unknown.

Rose Lawrence Peters, 1962, age 88.

and at the railway station across the way. Mama felt differently. She loved her new house and, sociable by nature, made up for all those years of isolation on the farm by joining a ladies' card club.

Papa died on September 10, 1940, aged 86, of myocarditis and gangrene in his right toes. After his death, Mama would remain active and in reasonably good health for many years. When she was in her eighties she sold the Danville house and bought another little house in Castro Valley, California so she could be near Ed, who retired there, and his family. Even when she could no longer work, she kept busy making doll clothes by hand for my granddaughter Kim Giambruni and Ed's daughter Rose Evelyn. Having retired, I moved in and took care of her for a year but finally she became so sick that she had to go into a nursing home. She liked the home, stayed cheerful right to the end, and was a favorite of the staff. Perhaps she enjoyed being taken care of after so many years of caring for others. And her lifetime of long sleeves and sunbonnets paid off. She told my daughter, proudly, that when the nurse bathed her she said she had "the skin of a baby." Ma died on March 14, 1967, aged 92, of heart failure.

Tiny quit high school after only a short time and worked on the farm. During World War I, when to his chagrin he was just under age to be a soldier, he worked for a time as a riveter in the shipyards, the needs of war giving him an excuse to escape the farm for a while. All my brothers couldn't wait to strike out for themselves, lured, no doubt, not only by freedom but by a weekly paycheck and an eight hour day. Tiny later

Tiny and Virgie Peters in their garden, Hayward, about 1955.

Tiny Peters, about 1957.

worked for the Caterpillar company, testing tractors if I'm not mistaken. He married Virginia Vieira, a widow with a young son, Howard, and they lived in her house in Hayward. He and Virgie had no children of their own.

For many years Tiny worked as a carpenter for Bradoff Construction Company, which built high quality homes in the Bay Area. He was a valued and highly versatile workman, good at almost anything he turned his hand to. With his mischievous smile, active imagination and colorful vocabulary of swear-words, he was also the natural center of every social group —family, friends, neighbors or fellow workers. Tiny died in 1962, aged 64, of lung cancer. He had been a lifelong chain smoker with a raspy voice and a smoker's cough, often

Horseshoe players outside the San Ramon Jail, 1927. Bert Peters second from right.

speaking with a cigarette dangling from his mouth. At his funeral, the church was packed with mourners and the apse and side aisles were banked high with wreaths and flowers in overwhelming profusion.

Bert was the only one of us who stayed close to home and the area where he grew up. The law making education compulsory through age 16 had not yet been enacted when he graduated from grammar school and, like Tiny, he chose not to go on to high school. For several years he continued to work on the farm. While Bert was still in grammar school he had taken a course in woodworking, or what was then called "manual training." He started by making a simple cylindrical stool, a tabouret, then graduated to a drop-top desk which always thereafter occupied a corner of our dining-room and served as a repository for bills, canceled checks, the Sears catalog and the like. During his years on the farm he continued to improve his woodworking skills, in part by helping Papa build a large storage barn for hay next to the horse barn. These skills would be a help to him when he came of age and was able to escape the drudgery of farm work. Given all the experience he had gained on the farm, he had no trouble getting hired as an apprentice carpenter in Danville and soon became skilled, continuing in that line of work for the rest of his life.

Bert always lived the same simple life: work, family and hanging out with his friends at the San Ramon Store, where Bill Ferreira had taken over from Harry Hurst. Before Bert married, Papa gave him a plot of land, a corner of the Home Ranch on the Danville side of the family orchard, on which he built a small Craftsman bungalow. He and his wife, Pearl, lived there until his death from cancer at age 38 in 1937. They had no children.

When Ed graduated from the University of California in 1926, with a major in English, he took a temporary job as a plumber's helper while he tried to decide what to do with his life. He knew he didn't want to be a teacher, a doctor, or a lawyer, the only careers he was vaguely familiar with, and unfortunately he had no career counseling. So, as he had enjoyed the R.O.T.C. classes at Berkeley, he signed up with a Marine Corps recruiter. Like all our family Ed was short, only about 5' 5" tall, and proportionately light in weight, so he met the Corps' size requirements only with some elaborate maneuvering. He was advised to go home and eat a big meal in order to meet the weight requirement, and when he appeared for the examination he combed his hair upright and stood slightly on his toes, probably while an indulgent doctor looked the other way.

During the early part of his career, Ed served in Nicaragua, Shanghai, and Hawaii. In 1941, he was in his quarters at Pearl Harbor when the Japanese bombers struck. For much of World War II he was assigned to the Quartermaster Corps but in the ferocious battle for Iwo Jima he finally got his wish to see action. Ed was awarded silver and bronze stars for his conduct there, one for the life-saving, on-the-spot idea of using portable flight-deck and runway materials to keep tanks from sinking into the sands when landing on the island. His last post was at Parris Island, North Carolina. Ed was a gentle, modest man, showing none of the toughness stereotypically associated with the Marines, yet he did very well, ending his military career as a Brigadier General, possibly the first, and certainly *one* of the first Portuguese-Americans to gain such a rank in the Corps. He loved the Marines, and said once that although boot camp was grueling, he had learned a lot about himself there and never regretted the experience. Years later, though, after his retirement, when he had renewed an early interest, he said he would have preferred geology if he had known when he was young that he could make a living at it.

Ed married Martha Wallace, with whom he had two children, Theodore (Ted) and Rose Evelyn (now Ram Dhan Kauer Khalsa). After his retirement to Castro Valley, he worked hard at his hobbies of woodworking, photography, jewelry making and gem cutting. Like all the other members of my immediate family except Evelyn, he was skillful with his hands. Ed organized Castro Valley Civil Defense in the 1950's and served for many years on the boards of the Fire Commission and the

Lt. Colonel Edward T. Peters, USMC, Honolulu, 1942.

Sanitary District. As a member of the Mineral and Gem Society he taught jewelry making to teenagers. He was much loved and admired in his community, and when he suffered the devastating blow of losing his son in Vietnam there was a great outpouring of sorrow and support. Ted had enlisted as a Marine private, keeping his father's rank secret. On April 7, 1969 he was shot and killed by a sniper while on reconnaissance patrol, less than five weeks after he landed in Vietnam. He was 19. Ed himself would die of bladder cancer on August 26, 1976, aged 73.

Evelyn followed Ed and me to the University of California, where she too worked as a family helper to help pay her way. Like me, and like her daughter Sylvia later, she majored in

Spanish at Berkeley. She was a high school teacher in the little town of Loyalton, California for a year or two, then married Herbert Hollis and settled in Berkeley. Together they founded and ran the University Electric store. Sylvia was their only child.

Ev was a skilled gardener and her big double yard was the beauty spot of her Berkeley neighborhood. True to Mama's description of her as "particular," she was also a meticulous housekeeper. Her house had been built by the contractor Tiny worked for, with Tiny on hand to see that everything was done to his high standards of workmanship. In later years she filled her lovely home with Japanese antiques, some bought on her travels abroad. Ev died on December 17, 1993, aged 86, after several years of progressively worsening Alzheimer's disease, the cruelest, most unsuitable disease imaginable for someone with her quick mind and perfectionist tendencies.

As for me, I enjoyed the university though sometimes I found it hard to earn my keep and still find enough time for my studies. Although we girls didn't get our way paid, as Ed did, Mama helped us as much as she could. She increased her flock of chickens and sold eggs to pay for our books, tuition and clothes, and sometimes a homemade dress would arrive in the mail. I always took some sort of summer job. One year I worked cutting fruit in a cannery with my sister-in-law Adeline Peters, Joe's wife, later in a bookstore, and as a movie usherette.

I majored in Spanish at Berkeley, planning to teach. I have always loved languages and since my retirement I have studied the Romance languages French, Italian and Portuguese on my own, and a little German as well. At the university I studied botany, philosophy, history, English and art. I took a tennis class and, more important, became a good swimmer, an activ-

Evelyn Peters Hollis in her Berkeley garden, c. 1945.

ity which I still enjoy. And I went to afternoon tea dances, where I met my future husband.

At the end of my junior year I dropped out of the university to marry Carol Emery. Later, when I was awaiting the birth of a baby, Mama sent me a complete layette. I cried when I got it because times were hard then and we were still struggling to scrape up money for the clinic bill. We lived for nine years in the state of Washington, where my husband's family was located. Then, after a divorce, I moved with my daughter, Helen, to San Francisco in 1938.

There had never been a divorce in our Catholic family and I dreaded telling my parents. I asked Tiny to speak to them first, to prepare them in advance. But I needn't have worried;

Carol Emery, Helen Emery and Rose Peters Emery at Lake Sammamish, Washington, 1928.

they made no fuss at all. Pa just said to Tiny, "Tell her to come home." However, I was determined to make my own way, so I borrowed the money from Ma to take some art courses. Afterward, I worked as a free-lance commercial artist in San Francisco for about two years, doing fashion illustration and other ads. But the United States was still in the Great Depression. Work was scarce and what there was paid very little. I remember that my most regular assignments came from J.C. Penney's department store. Once I did a full page ad for them in a local newspaper. This consisted of a checkerboard of small, boxed pen drawings, about 3" square, of miscellaneous

Rose Peters Emery, San Francisco, 1941.

things such as a pair of shoes, a sweater, an ironing board, a lamp, some socks. To get it in on time I had to work nearly all night before the morning it was due. The pay was $10 for the entire page.

Since free-lance art work was so chancy, I decided in 1941 to take a job with A. Carlisle and Company, printers, for a regular salary. I worked there through the war years as a layout and paste-up artist, readying pages for printing by lithography.

When Helen graduated from high school in 1945 and enrolled at Berkeley, I decided to take a chance and try something else. I quit my job and went back to the university with my daughter to finish my degree and get a teaching credential. To pay my way I lived and worked as a housemother—they

Helen and Rose, both students at the University of California, at a student co-op wedding, 1946. Rose made the wedding cake.

were required in those days!—in a student cooperative. Helen lived in another co-op house. Later, having earned a teaching credential in Spanish and art, I taught in a high school in the small Bay Area town of Benicia, then in a junior high school in Richmond, California before retiring to San Francisco.

When my mother died she left the Home Ranch to her surviving children. None of us could farm it and eventually we were forced to sell because of the taxes. For years after that I was reluctant to revisit the old place, but recently I let my

Mt. Diablo at sunset, 1920.

daughter drive me out to see what had been done out there.

All those precious haunts of my early years have vanished. It used to be that when you climbed up to the top of our land you looked down over our rolling hills with their tree-lined creeks and out across a broad, fertile, grassy valley, a vast expanse of green in the cool months, tawny brown in the heat. The valley was broken only by the gravel road at the foot of the hills and the patch of dark green that was Meese's Grove, and was dotted here and there with an occasional farmhouse or giant oak or row of eucalyptus. Now housing subdivisions heavily planted with trees stretch into the distance and creep up the sides of Mt. Diablo.

Highway 680 closely parallels the length of San Ramon

Boulevard, as the old road is now called, and the steep part of the road that used to be called Peters' Hill has been smoothed down. Of course the house is gone, along with the horse barn, the cow barn, the outbuildings, the corral and the orchard. A development of hundreds of houses called Danville Ranch extends about two-thirds of the way up our hills. The houses are pleasant, if a little nondescript in design, and well-maintained. The subdivision is beautifully landscaped, in fact almost manicured. The houses have been sited along curving roads so the natural contours of the land are not totally obliterated, as is so often the case with developments. I was pleased to see that the gullies with their winter creeks are still there, though they have been deepened by building up their banks, perhaps for flood control, and are less beautiful than they used to be.

Above Danville Farms, just below the crown of the hills at the top of what was once our property, is a separate and far more expensive development called Peters Ranch Estates. So far, three very large, custom houses on big lots with views of the entire San Ramon Valley and Mount Diablo have been built, although a number of still-undeveloped lots are staked out.

The developments are certainly not the desecration I had feared, yet I was still sad to see them. No farmer will ever again take a crop from that fertile land where once stood great stacks of baled hay and neatly piled sacks of wheat. No sleek red cattle will feed our growing population. I closed my eyes to blot out the changes. I want to remember my family's farm as it was in 1915, a place of beauty, serenity and productive work, a varied playground for growing children.

I am 97 years old now and the I am the only one left of my childhood family. All the others are gone, my mother, my

Five generations, 2000: Rose Peters Emery; daughter Helen Emery Giambruni; granddaughter Kim Giambruni Kenin; great-grandson Joshua Murray; with great-great granddaughter Ella Rose Murray.

father, my eleven brothers and sisters, every last one of those who used to constitute my world. But I suppose I could now be called the matriarch of another family consisting of my daughter, my grandson and granddaughter and my great-grandson with their spouses and my two beautiful little great-great granddaughters, all of us participants in a new and very different world.

Luckily, except for being hard of hearing I am still healthy. I live alone, I can read, I can still walk up the steep hill to my apartment and take buses to get around, and until last year I did all my own housework. I have managed to keep my independence. Yet I know I'll never get over that feeling of loss and nostalgia—*saudades,* the Portuguese call it—for my childhood family and our beautiful land. Few others are living who actually remember the world the way it was then. Soon there will be none. I have written this memoir so every trace of what used to be will not have disappeared.

A Family Album

Rose's daughter Helen, winter 1928, Snoqualmie, Washington.

Rose and daughter Helen at Lake Sammamish, Washington, 1932.

Rose's nephews and niece: Howard Peters, Clarence Lemos, Nadine Peters, Elwin Lemos, 1932.

Family reunion, Danville, 1942. Kneeling, left to right: Rose, Annie, Evelyn, Tiny.
Standing: Mary, Louise, Joe, Ed, Rose Lawrence Peters, Frank, Frances.

Application photo for first teaching job, 1947.

With grandson Mark Giambruni, Santa Cruz, CA, 1948.

Grandson Mark Giambruni, 1951.

Granddaughter Kim Giambruni, 1952.

With granddaughter Kim Giambruni, Santa Cruz, 1954.

Tiny and Ed Peters, Castro Valley, California, about 1960.

In camp on a fishing trip above Yosemite with Tiny and friends, about 1955.

Evelyn, 1962.

Picking apples, Santa Cruz, 1974.

With great-grandson Joshua Murray, 1975.

In the Tuileries Gardens, Paris, 1976.

Goofing around, Santa Cruz, 1979.

Grandson Mark Giambruni, 1979.

Kim Giambruni, Sag Harbor, N.Y., 1985

Joshua Murray and Rose, 1991.

Distant cousins at their home in Beira, São Jorge Island, the Azores, 1992.

Rose, 1996.

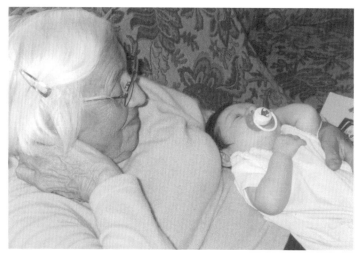

With great-great granddaughter Zoe Kathleen Murray, 2002.

Peters family picnic, Hayward, 2002.With niece Sylvia Carroll, left, and Helen.

Peters family picnic, Hayward, 2002. Rose's nieces Viva Denise (Denny) Bell and Gertrude Rodriguez, with Gertrude's son Bob.

Celebrating Rose's 97th birthday, 2002, on the beach at Pescadero, California. With Helen, left, and niece Sylvia Carroll.